ESL and Digital Video Integration: Case Studies

EDITED BY JIA LI, NICOLAS GROMIK, AND NICHOLAS EDWARDS

Typeset in ITC New Baskerville and Optima
by Capitol Communications, LLC, Crofton, Maryland USA
and printed by Gasch Printing, LLC, Odenton, Maryland USA

TESOL International Association
1925 Ballenger Avenue
Alexandria, Virginia 22314 USA
Tel 703-836-0774 • Fax 703-836-7864

Publishing Manager: Carol Edwards
Copyeditor: Sarah J. Duffy
Cover Design: Citrine Sky Design

TESOL Book Publications Committee
John I. Liontas, Chair

Maureen S. Andrade	Joe McVeigh
Jennifer Lebedev	Gail Schafers
Robyn L. Brinks Lockwood	Lynn Zimmerman

Project overview: John I. Liontas and Robyn L. Brinks Lockwood
Reviewers: Denise Mussman and Genevieve Leung

ISBN 9781931185783
Library of Congress Catalog No. 2012954365

Dedication

To all teachers and students who approach the teaching and learning of English as a nonnative language with unbounded imagination and creativity through technology integration.

Contents

Preface

It is a privilege to write a Preface for this inspirational book. In its chapters, we relive the experiences of learners and teachers who have used emerging technologies of literacy, particularly involving the visual medium, to create cultural artifacts that embody their insights, knowledge, aesthetic experiences, and critical analyses of social realities. These educational experiences involve the generation, sharing, and mobilization of knowledge in ways that stand in stark contrast to the one-way transmission of information and skills that has been the traditional *modus operandi* of schools.

In these pages, we also see glimpses of the future of teaching and learning, not just for English language learners (ELLs), but for all learners. We are rapidly approaching a tipping point where multimedia digital presentation of curriculum will replace textbooks. This process is being driven by simple economics rather than by the increased affordances for teaching and learning intrinsic to these digital devices. As tablets, netbooks, cell phones, and other forms of information and communication technologies (ICT) drop in price and, in more affluent countries, become as universally accessible as televisions are today, it will become increasingly more economical to provide students with digital access than to continue the printing and distribution of hard-copy resources.

Caution, however, is in order before we proclaim the emergence of a more enlightened digitally mediated educational future. It is appropriate to recall Larry Cuban's (2001) description of computers in the classroom as "oversold and underused" as he reflected on the fact that massive spending on technology in North American and European schools during the late 1980s and 1990s resulted in no measurable increase in school achievement. Part of the reason computers were "underused" was that access to the computers themselves and to the Internet was frequently limited, particularly in schools serving low-income students, and the equipment itself was often unreliable in performance. These hardware issues seem likely to be resolved within the next decade as relatively inexpensive hand-held devices with Internet access become ubiquitous.

However, less easily resolved are the pedagogical issues that have played at least an equal role in limiting the impact of ICT in the recent past. The pedagogical issue can be stated quite simply (see Cummins, 2004, and Cummins, Brown, & Sayers, 2007, for reviews): *Regardless of how powerful or user-friendly the ICT is, it will exert minimal impact on teaching and learning when it is implemented only within a transmission orientation to pedagogy.*

Numerous educational theorists have drawn distinctions similar to those between *transmission, social constructivist,* and *transformative* orientations to pedagogy. Briefly stated, colleagues and I (e.g., Skourtou, Kourtis-Kazoullis, & Cummins, 2006) have conceptualized these different orientations as nested within each other, reflecting the relative narrowness of their curricular focus. *Transmission orientations* are concerned simply to transmit information and skills articulated in the curriculum directly to students. *Social constructivist* pedagogy incorporates this narrow focus on the curriculum but broadens it to include the development among students of higher-order thinking abilities based on teachers and students co-constructing knowledge and understanding. Finally, *transformative* approaches broaden the focus still further by emphasizing the relevance not only of transmitting the curriculum and constructing knowledge but also of promoting social awareness and critical literacy among students.

Within the context of these three broad pedagogical orientations, we can ask whether the powerful affordances of emerging forms of ICT will push schools, particularly those serving low-income and ELL students, to expand their instructional focus beyond transmission of information and skills; or will the persistence of transmission approaches and intensive standardized testing stifle the efforts of progressive educators to enable low-income and ELL students to use these powerful tools to generate knowledge and engage in critical literacy? Obviously, time will tell. However, the projects and theoretical discussions in this book, together with descriptions of similar projects elsewhere (e.g., Hull & Katz, 2006), do enable us to sketch the pedagogical deep structure that will determine the success of technology-mediated teaching and learning activities.

THE POWER OF NEW TECHNOLOGIES

Constructs that are clearly operating in the case studies to enhance the power of new technologies for developing language and (multi)literacy skills are parallel to those that have emerged in syntheses of the research on print literacy development for ELL students in more typical school contexts (see Cummins, 2011; Cummins & Early, 2011):

- *Engaged participation* in (multi)literacy tasks and projects is key to the development of competence. As John Guthrie (2004, p. 8) noted with respect to the research on the centrality of engaged participation for all forms of human performance, including literacy achievement: "certainly some initial lessons are valuable for driving a car or typing on a keyboard but expertise spirals upward mainly with engaged participation."

- *Scaffolding* of both input (comprehension) and output (production) plays a crucial instructional role. For example, the various forms of readily available graphic supports in digital media (images, videos, drawings, etc.) facilitate participation; additionally, writing initially in the home language can help students transition to English writing (with the help of both human supports and technological translation tools). The role of these "external" scaffolding supports is similar to their role in supporting ELL students' learning in regular classrooms, but the scaffolding available in a digital environment is abundant and multidimensional (as documented in chapters in this volume) in ways that are typically not the case in classroom contexts.

- The projects undertaken by students in the case studies connect to their past, present, and future lives in ways that are virtually impossible in a transmission-oriented instructional environment. Students' background knowledge is activated as they engage in creating new meanings and insights. They are encouraged to pursue tasks and projects that interest them and to incorporate their knowledge and interests (e.g., in popular culture) into their productions. The projects in the case studies also stimulate students to use their imaginations to envisage new possibilities (e.g., through writing poetry or exploring solutions to social problems). These *connections to students' lives* operate as "internal" scaffolds that enable students to perform beyond their current levels of competence.

- The case studies document how participation in digital meaning making *affirmed students' identities* and enabled them to develop what Patrick Manyak (2004) has termed *identities of competence*. Although *identity* is a term that rarely appears in educational policy documents or in research reviews focused on students' academic achievement, there is extensive research documenting its centrality to academic engagement, particularly for students from low-income and racialized communities (see Cummins & Early, 2011). An implication of this research, which applies equally to regular classroom contexts, is that students will engage actively with literacy only to the extent that such engagement is identity-affirming. In this regard, creative writing and other forms of cultural production (e.g., art, drama, video creation) assume particular importance as *expressions* of identity, *projections* of identity into new social spheres, and *re-creation* of identity as a result of feedback from and dialogue with multiple audiences. We have used the term *identity text* to capture essential aspects of this process. Students invest their identities in the creation of texts which can be written, spoken, signed, visual, musical, dramatic, or combinations in multimodal form. The identity text then holds a mirror up to students in which their identities are reflected back in a positive light (Cummins & Early, 2011).

In conclusion, the research documented in this volume is important and powerful because it describes (a) how the pedagogical affordances of digital technologies promoted engaged participation in language and literacy learning on the part of ELL students and (b) the extent to which academic outcomes were superior to those typically observed in more traditional pedagogical environments (the Li and McComb case study in this volume is a particularly compelling example). Obviously, these findings cannot be generalized to other contexts—no such claim is being made. However, they do establish phenomena that require explanation and any theory of teaching and learning that cannot account for these findings must be modified. Two of the explanatory constructs which I have highlighted in this Preface, namely, *engaged participation* and *identity affirmation*—are largely absent from the transmission orientations to teaching and learning currently operating in many schools serving low-income students. I would argue that neglect of these explanatory constructs represents a major reason why almost 50 years of compensatory transmission-oriented schooling for low-income and racialized students in the United States have produced such disappointing returns on human and economic investment. My hope is that the emerging technologies of literacy, vividly evoked in this volume, will reduce the pedagogical divide between affluent and poor students and shift the instructional focus in schools towards social constructivist and transformative approaches.

Jim Cummins, PhD
University of Toronto

Acknowledgments

Since the inception of the book, 5 years have flown by. We are grateful to our contributors, whose dedication and perseverance has been critical in making this book possible.

I would like to thank my coeditors—Nicolas Gromik for his initiative and work on the book proposal, and Nick Edwards for his detailed attention in editing the manuscripts. Special thanks also go to Yan Wang, a graduate student at Boston College, for her assistance in preparing the references.

With sincere gratitude, I would like to acknowledge the support of Fulbright Canada in sponsoring my 2011–2012 Fulbright Research scholarship at the Harvard Graduate School of Education, which enabled me to complete major revisions of the manuscripts.

My coeditors and I owe a significant debt to Dr. Catherine Snow, whose insights during our discussions about the alignment between language and literacy learning outcomes and instructional technology greatly shaped the focus of the volume. Her support also provided invaluable opportunities for Nick Edwards and me to work together intensively on the volume.

We would like to pay tribute to Dr. Jim Cummins and Dr. Mark Warschauer for their respective works on multiliteracies in multilingual contexts and technology-based language instruction. Their contributions in these fields have been inspirational to the endeavors presented in this volume.

We wish to thank Dr. Tim Collins and two anonymous reviewers for generously contributing their time and expertise to reviewing the manuscripts. We are also grateful to our copy editor, Sarah J. Duffy, for her careful reading of the manuscripts and her helpful suggestions and corrections. Finally, we would like to express our deep appreciation to Carol Edwards, our publisher at TESOL, for her patience and professionalism. It has been a great honour and pleasure for us to work with her and her team, who assisted in bringing this book to fruition.

Jia Li, PhD
University of Ontario Institute of Technology
Canada-U.S. Fulbright Scholar (2011–2012)
Harvard Graduate School of Education

CHAPTER 1

TESOL and Digital Video Media Integration in the Classroom: Introduction

Jia Li

DIGITAL VIDEO MEDIA AND LINGUISTICALLY DIVERSE STUDENTS

In 1992, TESOL published its first book addressing the use, selection, and production of video for English language classrooms (Stempleski & Arcario, 1992). Since the publication of this volume, video technology has advanced considerably; the world in which we live is marked by the widespread availability of inexpensive recording and editing devices and programs as well as the ease of publishing and accessing videos online. Digital camera functionality embedded in cell phones has become increasingly ubiquitous. According to research from Strategy Analytics (Shah, 2011) and InfoTrends (2008), it was estimated that worldwide camera phone sales exceeded 1 billion units in 2011 and would exceed 1.3 billion units in 2012. Video editing programs that support major video formats can now enable novice users to create professional-looking videos and motion pictures that may include numerous innovative animation techniques, visual and audio effects, text comments, and subtitles.

Nowadays, digital media technologies are pervasive in people's everyday lives. This is most evident among younger people. For example, a survey by InfoTrends (2007) shows that most 13–24 year olds in the United States use camera phones for taking pictures or videos on a daily basis, and they were satisfied with the features and ease of use. As of February 2011, YouTube had 490 million users worldwide, generating an estimated 92 billion page views each month. People spend approximately 2.9 billion hours on YouTube each month, and 48 hours of video are uploaded every minute (*Statistics*, n.d.). The younger generations, which include many who have already chosen to live much of their social lives in virtual space, often share and exchange instant messages with embedded videos and pictures via blogs and websites such as Facebook and Twitter. Social media–related YouTube statistics show that, on average, more than 400 tweets per minute contain YouTube links. Meanwhile, on Facebook more than 150 years' worth of YouTube videos are watched every single day (*Statistics*, n.d.).

For the past decade, literature regarding the digital divide has raised concerns about equal access to digital technology among linguistically and culturally diverse students. The "digital divide" refers to the fact that historically underserved segments of society, including the urban poor, new immigrants, and those in remote rural communities, have little access to the new information and communication technologies whose use by mainstream students is growing rapidly. An earlier study conducted by Mossberger, Tolbert, and Stansbury (2003) in the United States showed that teens who had high-speed Internet access were more likely to be White and had college-educated parents with annual household incomes higher than $50,000, although the "digitally disadvantaged" lower income and minority teens often shared many of the same positive orientations toward technology as their more privileged counterparts. Mossberger et al.'s results also show that African Americans are more positive in their attitudes toward technology than their White counterparts in many respects, contrary to public assumptions.

Recent data indicate a shift in the digital divide as a result of mobile technology, with cell phones leapfrogging connectivity roadblocks for low-income and minority populations. Teen smartphone owners in the lowest household income category are most likely to use their handset to go online (41% with income under $30,000 versus 23% over $75,000; Purcell, 2010). Studies of differences in youth media use by race and ethnicity reveal that minority youth in the United States spend about 1.5 hours more each day using their phones for activities such as watching videos and television than did White youth (Rideout, Foehr, & Roberts, 2010). Eighty-one percent of Hispanics have used a video-sharing site, compared to 76% of African Americans and 69% of non-Hispanic Whites (Moore, 2011). Although this may indicate that the digital divide is diminishing, and online video sharing popularity steadily grows, limited evidence is available of the pedagogical benefits of integrating digital technology into English language teaching practice. Two fundamental questions remain unanswered. Will ELLs be interested in learning English language skills through viewing or producing digital video? What learning outcomes will result from the integration of digital video into classroom instruction?

APPLICATION OF DIGITAL VIDEO MEDIA TO TESOL

As mentioned earlier, recent studies indicate an increasing utility and strong interest in digital media among diverse populations. The findings from a study in the United States (Li & Snow, 2012) show that urban middle school students expressed different levels of interest in using technology for language and literacy learning purposes. When surveyed about using four media platforms for learning (i.e., Facebook, YouTube, Twitter, and cell phone text messaging), the students were most interested in YouTube. More important, ELLs in the study were generally more interested in using these platforms for learning purposes than their native-English-speaking peers were. The difference in interest between the two groups in using YouTube for learning language and literacy skills was statistically significant, with ELLs again expressing greater interest (Li & Snow, 2012).

A growing body of articles has emerged documenting effective English language teaching practice that incorporates the viewing and production of video clips (e.g., Dhonau & McAlpine, 2002; Goldman, 1996; Rowland, 2007; Swaffer & Vlatten, 1997; Vanderplank, 1993). This literature reports on the findings of research that has specifically investigated the impact of video media on ESL and EFL students' identity confirmation, learning attitudes, and behavior (e.g., South, Gabbitas, & Merrill, 2008) and assessing learning outcomes in terms of English language skills (e.g., Chen, 2011; Chung, 1999, 2002; Hanley, Herron, & Cole, 1995; Markham, Peter, & McCarthey, 2001), pragmatic competence (e.g., Louw, Derwing, & Abbott, 2010), sociocultural knowledge (e.g., Herron, Cole, Corrie, & Dubreil, 1999), and critical analysis skills (e.g., Ajayi, 2012).

Some recent studies that directly address the development of specific language skills using video have had promising results. For instance, Wagner (2007, 2008, 2010) investigated the impact of video on the listening comprehension of adult ESL students. His quasi-experimental study (Wagner, 2010) reveals that nonverbal information in video texts contributed to students' enhanced performance in comprehending aural information relative to audio-only texts. Wagner uses his findings to make a convincing case for the validity of including video in the assessment of listening comprehension (see Chapter 9 in this book for a detailed review of Wagner's studies). Another study, by Louw et al. (2010), shows that a pedagogical intervention using video was effective in helping ESL professionals develop specific pragmatic skills and facilitate intercultural communication in the workplace through simulated job interviews. An automatic video and transcript synchronization system called SynctoLearn, developed by Chen (2011), was found to be helpful for EFL students. This system "uses speech recognition technologies to automatically synchronize voices in audios and videos with their respective transcripts" (p. 117), thus enabling students to make better use of authentic videos and reducing their cognitive loads and anxiety levels. Chen's research compared two student groups watching video with and without using synchronized subtitles, and his findings show that the former outperformed the latter in comprehending the video content and learning vocabulary items.

Building on the existing literature, the present volume provides TESOL educators and researchers with reflections and insights based on firsthand experiences in teaching practice and research from a variety of contexts that integrate video.

ORGANIZATION OF THE BOOK

The book consists of nine chapters, including the present introduction chapter and a final chapter that reviews research on the use of video with ELLs in the United States. Chapters 2–8 report on original case studies, all reflecting on effective and engaging ways that teachers and researchers in several countries have incorporated video, including motion pictures, into their teaching practice to enhance instruction for ESL and EFL learners. These case studies are based on sociolinguistic and second language acquisition theories; as a whole, they demonstrate that ELLs in the 21st century need to adapt social practices for communicating with digital tools in multiple social and cultural contexts, that is, to "navigate, make meaning from, and be critical of more than print modalities" (Toohey & Dagenais, this volume). Under these circumstances, interacting with and creating video via multimedia might be among the best means of enabling ELLs to learn language skills in an engaging, enjoyable, and meaningful way.

Chapters in this volume are arranged by alternating topics across countries collectively connecting to the major theme, so readers can start with any chapter following their personal interests. The contributions made by international authors reflect their TESOL teaching experience and research results, applying digital video to language education in Asia, the Middle East, North America, and South America. The volume includes research reports with a focus on pedagogical implications as well as documentation of action research conducted by TESOL classroom practitioners—all in consideration of robust theories of language acquisition and learner motivation. Though the format of each chapter is flexible, all of the case studies comprise references to prior studies, descriptions and evaluations of actual classroom experiences integrating digital video, and the impact of these experiences on teaching and learning. An overview is given to introduce each chapter's pedagogical significance, research contributions, or both.

In response to the rapidly evolving and digitally based nature of contemporary communication, Lotherington and Sinitskaya Ronda in Chapter 2 propose to revise the concept of communicative competence, going beyond reading, writing, listening, and speaking in terms of printed texts, to also include navigating, designing, linking, programming, and sharing dynamic, multimodal texts. Their case studies involve two groups of linguistically diverse first-generation immigrant learners in urban neighborhoods in Canada, showcasing how communicative competence can be redefined for digital multimedia environments in the context of the English language classroom—how the use of screens can create fundamentally different language learning spaces. One of their projects involved diverse 4th- and 5th-grade students using digital media to interpret and construct the abstract quality of beauty in a personally meaningful way; the other engaged 11th-grade students in learning English with Facebook. The authors introduce the notion of *intermedial flows of meaning* (Elleström, 2010) to address the complexities of communicative competence in multimedia contexts.

Chapters 3 and 4 focus on how video provides opportunities for the expression of cultural knowledge and identity construction among ELLs. In Chapter 3, Toohey and Dagenais describe three videomaking projects by Canadian teacher candidates with diverse ELLs in a Canadian school, with Tibetan children learning English in a boarding school in northern India, and with Spanish-speaking learners attending bilingual English and Zapotec lessons at a community library in Mexico. The chapter focuses on how video affords opportunities for learners to represent their own cultural knowledge and practices in ways that would be impossible in typical classroom print and verbal tasks. The findings demonstrate that videomaking is a promising classroom practice that, if embraced by young students, could potentially promote language learning.

Chapter 4 presents case studies in which Eamer and Hughes explore middle school ELLs' knowledge of digital media to support their language learning and adaptation to life in Toronto, Canada. Eamer and Hughes describe ELLs with limited English proficiency using multimodal forms of expression—images, music, and narrative in both English and their native language—to author digital poems and stories. These digitally authored texts provide the students with a forum to construct, negotiate, and communicate their identities as new Canadians. As a result, the authors argue that multimodality can facilitate ELLs' learning of a variety of vital English language skills, such as vocabulary building and organizing ideas for writing and speaking.

Although the development of language skills is certainly an important aspect of all work presented in this volume, such skill development becomes a more primary focus in Chapters 5–8. In Chapter 5, Yeh describes a photostory project that engaged undergraduate EFL students in Taiwan in creating motion pictures by combining visual arts and English lyrics to tell stories that were visually and emotionally captivating. Yeh illustrates project procedures that effectively encourage students to apply their language skills by integrating personal experiences with an appreciation of music and the arts.

In Chapter 6, Li and McComb document the positive impact of a filmmaking project on the English language learning outcomes, and particularly vocabulary acquisition, of undergraduate ELLs in a Canadian university. The chapter shows how filmmaking that is based on carefully written scripts and allows for personal interpretation of characters can create optimal opportunities for students to develop English communication skills and acquire vocabulary. Li and McComb provide a pragmatic approach for motivating linguistically and culturally diverse ELLs while nurturing more interactive learning in multimedia environments.

In Chapter 7, Cunningham reports on a project that enhanced Japanese EFL undergraduates' oral English proficiency and critical thinking skills by involving them in deconstructing advertisements and creating their own digital commercials. Cunningham's study intends to bridge the gap between language acquisition and critical thinking that can occur in EFL classes by taking advantage of multimedia venues to promote critical thinking while at the same time ensuring that students learn to communicate effectively using spoken English.

Chapter 8 also focuses on the use of video production to promote effective oral communication. Gromik reports on a case study conducted in Qatar, describing Arab female undergraduate students' use of cell phone technology as well as their perceptions of using the cell phone video recording feature to enhance their speaking abilities in an academic English program. Gromik found that inquiry-based video production activities, which required students to explain technical processes and express opinions verbally using academic English language, were most suitable and beneficial for EFL learners at advanced levels of proficiency.

To complement the case studies throughout the book, Chapter 9 provides a thematic literature review of 11 research reports on the use of digital video as an educational medium for ELLs in the United States. Edwards, et al. focus on how video-based activities can impact various language learning outcomes for ESL students. They identify some important characteristics of video-based projects that may be particularly beneficial for improving learners' language skills, such as the richness of contextual information and the availability of English captions.

CONCLUSIONS

Today's students' abilities to take in, learn, and process information are dramatically different from those of previous generations. To effectively enhance ESL students' various language skills, pragmatic knowledge, and cultural competence in order to assist their effective communication in English and adjustment to life in English-medium countries, English language educators need to leverage digital media technology to create fluid, enjoyable, interactive, and collaborative learning environments. It should come as no surprise that digital video technology is of particular interest to ELLs; students are drawn to its visual appeal and vibrant creative potential. Teachers can use video to contextualize their lessons and provide students with authentic language experiences that would be otherwise unavailable in the classroom. As demonstrated in this volume, video can be an effective and powerful tool for teaching and learning English. It has provided many new opportunities for extending students' attention spans, teaching them challenging language skills, eliciting creativity, and supporting learning with social scaffolding (Gee, 2003, 2004; Gee, Hull, & Lankshear, 1996; Vygotsky, 1978).

This volume contests a notion that used to be widely held—that the use of technology in language education is predominantly limited to computer-assisted language learning and online distance learning. Working in the context of the face-to-face English language classroom, the authors report on data-driven teaching practices and classroom-based research that affirm, and in some cases broaden, theories relevant to teaching and learning a second language. However, we are aware of limitations due to methodological constraints such as small sample sizes and qualitative self-report measures. Therefore, in terms of future directions for teaching and research in this area, we believe "more large-scale, longitudinal research with quantitative measures is needed to further clarify the nature of the relationship between specific instructional uses of digital video and language learning outcomes" (Edwards et al., this volume).

Second, although the constantly advancing functionality of digital media may foster an enthusiasm for using such media in the English language classroom, this may not necessarily lead to positive learning outcomes. Thus, procedures and techniques for incorporating digital video media into the classroom should be carefully defined to promote implementation that is well aligned with research-driven learning principles (C. Snow, personal communication, February 16, 2010).

Third, because video demonstrates a great capacity for ELLs to see, hear, and read (with captions) the target language simultaneously in contextually rich environments, the impact of video on a broader range of language skills beyond listening, vocabulary, and pragmatics needs to be assessed. This particularly includes the development of reading and writing skills by integrating digital video technologies for ELLs.

Finally, the quality of video used for TESOL purposes can be further improved, with additional features to support learning and instruction, such as annotations and interactive glossaries. We hope that this volume can inspire more thoughtful work in this area, including innovative interventions using well-defined pedagogical principles and research with robust methods.

As the teaching of nonnative language and literacy continues to adapt to the fast pace of change in literate communication, it is important for TESOL professionals to observe both (1) the shift from the largely paper-based communicative competencies of the 20th century to the largely screen-based communications of the 21st century (Lotherington & Sinitskaya Ronda, this volume) and (2) the benefits of keeping instruction aligned with the interests of today's technologically savvy students (Cummins, Brown, & Sayers, 2007; Warschauer, 2011).

CHAPTER 2

Revisiting Communicative Competence in the Multimedia ELT Classroom

Heather Lotherington and Natalia Sinitskaya Ronda

As the teaching of language and literacy attempts to adapt to the furious pace of change in literate communication, teachers are caught between the paper-based communicative competencies of the 20th century and the digitally mediated, screen-based communications of the 21st century. Dynamic environments for contemporary communication are evolving rapidly; theories of language, literacy, and communication need to catch up.

This chapter considers how communicative competence can be reshaped for digital multimedia environments in the context of the English language teaching (ELT) classroom. We propose a revised approach to communicative competence which goes beyond reading, writing, listening, and speaking in terms of static texts, to consider navigating, designing, linking, programming, and sharing dynamic multimodal texts.

Examples of the use of screens to create language learning spaces are taken from two school contexts in Toronto, Canada, both of which involve first-generation immigrant learners in urban neighbourhoods which are characterized by high linguistic and cultural diversity. The first project takes place in an elementary school where 4th- and 5th-grade students interpreted the abstract quality *beauty* from different sensory perspectives after reading *Just Ella* (Haddix, 1999), a contemporary feminist version of the traditional narrative *Cinderella*. Students worked across languages, cultural backgrounds, and media to build and express a concept of beauty that was personally meaningful to them—a concept that questioned predominant pop culture ideals of beauty. The second example is taken from a project involving 47 Grade 11 high school students learning English with Facebook. The emergent flows of meaning are discussed through examples of how, in the multimedia environment of Facebook, participants were able to access and create a variety of texts and construct their own understanding of the course material from them.

A BAD FIT: DIGITAL MEDIA AND PRINT-BASED COMPETENCIES

The pursuit of *communicative competence* in the 1970s and 1980s led to the development the communicative language teaching (CLT) approach which has become normative in ELT. However, the conceptualization of communicative competence at the heart of CLT, as Leung (2005) notes, has not evolved over time with "ethnographic sensitivities and sensibilities" (p. 119). In this chapter we argue that pedagogical interpretations of communicative competence have similarly not evolved with the *technical media* of communication (Elleström, 2010)—the material surfaces on which we read and write. Though we have incorporated digitally mediated communication into our day-to-day social practices, we have not kept pace in the ELT classroom, where vestigial resistance to digital genres resides in language teaching that prioritizes paper-based language norms. These norms shape classroom practices and teaching materials, and influence professional qualification programs. The importance of succeeding in standardized tests in various ELT contexts tends to further funnel language learning towards prescriptive, paper-based norms.

As social literacy practices migrate from the page to the screen, ELT professionals need to rethink what communicative competence entails. This rethinking requires a reconceptualization of the technical media involved in communication. Elleström (2010) defines technical media as "tangible devices needed to materialize instances of media types" (p. 12). We can visualize these technical media as the paper on which we write with a pen, the small screens of smartphones that we check on a regular basis, and the large screens for projections at the front of a classroom. Contemporary communication is conducted with a variety of technical media that were not in existence when communicative competence was initially theorized.

The screen as a technical medium of communication in second language teaching is, of course, not new. Since the 1960s, ELT has included educational television and, subsequently, video presentations for second language learning (see, e.g., Corder, 1966; Eisenstein, Shuller, & Bodman, 1987; Handscombe, 1975). However, the centralized teacher-controlled television screen featuring a commercial video product has kaleidoscoped into interactive screens of varied shapes and sizes, including interactive whiteboards, tablet computers, digital readers, and miniature portable devices, such as smartphones and MP3 players. These interactive screens enable agentive learning—they are not limited to the earlier one-way audience viewing of television screens. Even an inexpensive digital camera has the potential to both capture and replay a short video, so the student, once only a consumer of video presentations, is now also a producer of such materials (Jenkins, 2008). This creates a new role and a new set of competencies: that of "prosumer" (Toffler, 1980, p. 27).

In this social environment, English language learners (ELLs) require, at a minimum, the language and literacy competencies to enable online communication. The conventions around email, for instance, differ substantially from those used in letter writing; similarly, web navigation is vastly different from library research. Elementary computer skills are now an essential element in text building and editing, which often requires the use of software such as PowerPoint or web-based programs such as Prezi, or even in reading in the case of *apps* (downloadable programs), which can be used for downloading and reading e-books. Participation in social networking sites, such as Facebook or LinkedIn, opens up new dimensions in communication by linking *friends* one may never have met in person and engaging multimedia as a fundamental part of this communication. The screen interface facilitates communication where language is woven into multimodal texts encompassing a variety of semiotic resources. The potential for collaborative authorship is created in interactive text-building environments, such as *wikis* (websites that allow any user to modify and add content), and the resulting texts are dynamic.

These new digital sites of communication, accessed through screen interfaces, call on new communicative competencies. This chapter presents the thesis that we need to revisit—and, in the words of Bolter and Grusin (1999), *remediate*—communicative competence to account for the complex communicative demands of the digital era. We discuss this imperative against the backdrop of two case studies of linguistically heterogeneous students learning English with and through screen-based activities in different educational settings. We begin with a discussion of mid-20th century theories of digital culture as an evolutionary step from print culture. We then review the notion of communicative competence, which emerged as a guiding aim in second language instruction in the 1970s and 1980s. We build a case for reviewing the scope of communicative competence in the 21st century, based on the continued evolution of literate communication practices with changing technical media. We close with an invitation to TESOL professionals to reconsider the boundaries of ELT practices, and the competencies required for successful acquisition of contemporary communicative agency.

This is a critical step for teachers because formal education is based on literacy. Language learning is accessed largely through text, and texts are changing. Languages can be encoded and accessed in contemporary communicative media that enable multiple modes within a single text, that link multimodal texts beyond the paper borders of a book, and that enable dynamic interactive texts. The implications for teachers, accustomed to basing language standards and styles on static alphabetic text, are immense.

FROM PRINT TO DIGITAL CULTURE

McLuhan (1964), in describing the evolution of print culture into electronic culture a half century ago, credited the printed book as being "the first teaching machine and also the first mass produced commodity" (p. 174). McLuhan (1962) assigned the concept of grammar to print culture: "Typography extended its character to the regulation and fixation of languages" (p. 229), noting that "nobody ever made a grammar error in a non-literate society" (p. 238). His prediction of an "automation age" (1964, p. 346) evolving from changes in cultural communication media made possible with electricity is encapsulated in the over-quoted sound bite "the medium is the message" (1964, p. vii). In McLuhan's (1962) futuristic vision, the individual is extended through electronic media into a globally connected nervous system, wherein "the new electronic interdependence recreates the world in the image of a global village" (p. 31). In the digitally connected global era of the 21st century, we have arrived.

Ong (1980, 1982), writing on the complexities of literacy in the electronic age of the late 20th century, delineates a complex interaction between orality and literacy, describing "the new, secondary orality that surrounds us on radio and television" (1980, p. 198). His theory describes the nonlinearity of orality and literacy: Children learn to speak at home and then learn to read in school, but they are simultaneously exposed to scripted oral performances on radio and television, which follow from written text. The complex intermingling of oral and written literacies that Ong points to in the context of the electronic age is also identified in community literacy studies of the same era, which find complex interactions and exclusions in oral and literate behaviours and environments (Heath, 1983; Street, 1984). In Heath's (1983) research, schools are selectively attentive to middle-class mainstream language and literacy practices. During this era, analyses of and approaches to communicative competence for second language teaching were being formulated (Canale, 1983; Canale & Swain, 1980; Savignon, 1972) to expand the educational paradigm of language as four linear and discrete skills: speaking–listening and reading–writing.

Communication has continued to evolve with revolutionary technological developments that have catapulted the global reading public into a cybernetic world. The changing focus from print to digital culture carries concomitant changes in the conception of, realization of, and access to discourse, texts, and education. McLuhan (1964) theorized a paradigm shift in learning, moving formal education away from the values of the Industrial Age and the slicing of knowledge into subject areas and towards integrated learning focusing on process. He warned, "Continued in their present patterns of fragmented unrelation, our school curricula will ensure a citizenry unable to understand the cybernated world in which they live" (p. 347).

During each cultural cycle in literacy history, literate communication has expanded socially and epistemologically. In the shift from print to digital culture that society has been undergoing over the past decades, literate communication has substantially slid off the page and onto the screen. As numerous eminent researchers have warned, education has not kept up (Cope & Kalantzis, 2009; Gee, 2004; Kellner, 2004; Kress, 2003; Lankshear & Knobel, 2006; New London Group, 1996).

COMMUNICATIVE COMPETENCE AND PRINT CULTURE

In the early 1980s, the major paradigm for second language teaching was shifting away from structuralism and attention to mastery of the language code towards communicative competence. A landmark paper by Canale and Swain (1980) explicated the emerging trend towards teaching language as social communication, with grammatical learning—previously the sole aim of second language learning—forming a component in an interdependent system which included the language system itself, the processing of communication in use, and its social contextualization. The theoretical roots of this pedagogical refocusing emerged from linguistic–sociolinguistic differences in the conception of what it means to know a language.

Hymes (1972) was one of a number of scholars who pointed to the lack of context in Chomsky's (1965, p. 3) construction of language competence which described the "ideal speaker–listener, in a completely homogeneous speech community." This delineation was assessed by Hymes as "almost a declaration of irrelevance" (p. 53). He reframed Chomsky's conception of language competence, which posed language learning in terms of grammatical competence as an innate, hardwired process, proposing a fuller description of communicative competence. Canale and Swain (1980) elucidated Hymes' conception of communicative competence as "the interaction of grammatical (what is formally possible), psycholinguistic (what is feasible in terms of human information processing), sociocultural (what is the social meaning or value of a given utterance), and probabilistic (what actually occurs) systems of competence" (p. 16).

Canale and Swain (1980) applied the theoretical notion of communicative competence to the teaching of French as a second language in Canada, considering both competence and performance:

> We have so far adopted the term "communicative competence" to refer to the relationship and interaction between grammatical competence, or knowledge of the rules of grammar, and sociolinguistic competence, or knowledge of the rules of language use. Communicative competence is to be distinguished from communicative performance, which is the realization of these competencies and their interaction in the actual production and comprehension of utterances (under general psychological constraints that are unique to performance). (p. 6)

Canale and Swain (1980) posited a set of five guiding principles for a communicative approach to second language teaching and testing, delineating (1) the minimal conditions for communicative competence as comprising grammatical, sociolinguistic, and strategic competencies, each of equitable importance; (2) the basis of a communicative approach being the learner's communicative needs; (3) the importance of meaningful and authentic communicative interaction with competent speakers; (4) the importance of importing the learner's first language competencies into second language learning; and (5) the spreading of language learning across the curriculum to include grammatical study and sociocultural learning in addition to communicative acquisition and practice in the second language (pp. 27–28).

Canale and Swain (1980) proposed a basic framework outlining the boundaries of grammatical, sociolinguistic, and strategic competencies. Canale (1983) refined this framework towards the teaching and testing of French as a second language in Ontario, extending communicative competence to include discourse as well as grammatical (knowledge of formal aspects of the language), sociolinguistic (knowledge of how to produce and interpret utterances for social meaning), and strategic competencies (strategies used to ensure effective communication and compensate for communicative breakdowns). These competencies could be taught and tested for in terms of the four language skills: "listening comprehension, speaking, reading comprehension and writing" (Canale, 1983, p. 21).

These skills corresponded to the media of the time: speech, and its mechanized (e.g., over a telephone) and recorded forms (i.e., printed text, audio recording, and video recording). Recorded forms of speech were static texts that did not permit interaction or customization and manifested only limited multimedia design (e.g., layout and illustrations in books). Current communications media extend linguistic processing beyond the traditional four skills paradigm, requiring hybridized language use in new texts and discourses, such as mobile phone "txting," which includes features of both reading and writing and is neither (Lotherington, 2004); gaming, which requires interactive, problem-solving processing and participation, and permits customization or *modding* (Gee, 2008); and social media platforms, in which dynamic, multimodal, interactive texts are created and shared. Given that digital texts are interactive and dynamic, the term *writing* (in the traditional sense of stringing words together on a static page) is inadequate to describe the creation of such texts.

The distinction between communicative competence and communicative performance formed a substantial part of early discussions (Canale & Swain, 1980). However, the notion of communicative performance devolved into that of "actual communication," referring to the idea that "communicative competence is an essential part of actual communication but is reflected only indirectly" (Canale, 1983, p. 5). Cazden (1997) later argued that performance in fact precedes competence. This is also illustrated in digital gaming and social media, where learners jump into the site and learn to navigate it from within. We now find that performance is not the demonstration of competence, but the exploratory pursuit of it.

COMMUNICATIVE COMPETENCE AND DIGITAL CULTURE

How have the media of communication shifted in the digital age? As Lothering-ton (2004) notes, "the four-skill areas historically demarcated as reading, writing, speaking, and listening are artificial distinctions in digital communication where the borders between oral and written language are not clearly distinguishable. Communication via digital media includes synchronous and asynchronous connection possibilities" (p. 69).

The fluid, dynamic, interactive texts of the 21st century extend far beyond the technical media of teaching contexts in the 1970s and 1980s on which the communicative competencies for second language teaching and testing were theorized. Though teaching entails face-to-face communication, which is four-dimensional (4D), including the three spatial dimensions as well as time, the content for language study and the communicative competencies of the testing world rely heavily on flat 2D technical media of the paper-and-pencil era. Digitally mediated, multimodal communication takes place in 3D environments where time is a salient communicative dimension and in immersive virtual reality environments such as Second Life, which simulate a 4D experience by creating an illusory depth field. These multidimensional communicative interactions extend beyond the alphabetic in terms of reading and writing, and beyond the audience models of 20th century interactive speech. Social media such as Twitter are based on a one-to-many communicative model with an unknown and unknowable audience. This audience can take advantage of asynchronous connection to chatty communication of a sort that simply did not exist in the 1980s.

In digital media environments, communication requires multimedia competencies; scanning, listening, viewing, reading, writing, linking, navigating digitally, programming, and multimodal designing constitute a new communicative repertoire. Importantly, navigation can happen across physical and online platforms: Learners are copresent in the physical environment and synchronously or asynchronously present in the online environment. Multiple modes are combined to create multimedia experiences, where boundaries between conventional communicative competencies become blurred. Not only do writing and speaking blend—a chat online or a smartphone text message requires a literate interface but works at the speed of speech—but a multisensory experience is created where nonverbal means of communication (e.g., viewing, movement) interweave with verbal means of communication. Language teachers cannot continue to focus on outdated skills that describe only static print conventions when the resources students need to access language require dynamic, multimodal literacies: the ability to understand and create linked, multimedia texts.

As communication has moved off the page and onto the screen, the minimal unit of encoding has shifted from the letter to the pixel (Cope, Kalantzis, & Lankshear, 2005). This pixelization of communication moves the focus from language to multimedia; words, images, and sounds can be encoded digitally and combined to convey meaning. The implications for the communication landscape are profound: Meaning can be encoded in ways that are multidimensional, multimedia, portable, manipulable, and shareable. Social media platforms show this pixelized communication at work; sites such as Facebook and YouTube combine video, images, and verbal communication, all wrapped into a complex web of navigable digital space.

To create pixelized communication in digital environments where multiple media choices must be made requires new competencies. Grammatical competence must also include *multimodal grammar*: the extension of discourse grammar to the successful use of digital modes such as video, sound and image, or any combination of these. New genres emerge, throwing the established communicative dynamic into question. For example, *machinima*, a grassroots video genre, combines footage from video games with user-created narratives; Facebook includes still and moving images with short texts that invite comments, all posted along a timeline, as well as capacities for online chatting and messaging.

Sociolinguistic competence is challenged by new digital platforms. From Twitter to YouTube, communicative contexts emerge where traditional understandings of what is appropriate communication no longer apply. In Twitter, a communicative event is limited to 140 characters; on Facebook, the *Like* button has become a powerful means of communication used by individuals and organizations alike to grow a viewership, as demonstrated by the ubiquitous digital sticker: *Like us on Facebook*; and YouTube facilitates communication where video, not print, becomes the focal point. YouTube is not only a powerful social and entertainment platform; it is gaining momentum as a medium for innovative publishing. In her groundbreaking work publishing a YouTube-based collection, Juhasz (2011) coins the term *texteo* to describe a page in her publication "that expresses meaning through the integration of design, written text, and video."

Digital communication is increasingly collaborative, transcending geographical boundaries to create sites of communication that are not predicated on physical copresence. The Internet has given rise to never-before-seen collaborative opportunities: from Wikipedia, a bottom-up encyclopedia co-constructed by the digital public, to immersive gaming worlds in which participants from different physical locations around the globe can explore and work together. In a recent example of crowdsourcing, a process of collaborative problem solving by a dispersed online community, video gamers solved a molecular puzzle that might one day lead to finding a cure for AIDS (Boyle, 2011).

These new technical media of communication provide English language learners with the tools to learn by doing. Learning thus becomes agentive and performative. Learners' L1 multiliterate competencies can provide a framework for positive discourse transfer in second language learning. For example, learners familiar with social networking sites such as Facebook can focus on English grammatical, alphabetic, and sociolinguistic norms as well as socioculturally appropriate design factors when using these sites.

MEDIATION

In new digital contexts, different media connect in novel ways, creating new communicative opportunities and requiring new strategies. Understanding the relationships between different media can help us examine challenges to notions of communicative competence. Bolter and Grusin (1999) propose a notion of *remediation* to tackle the nature of proliferating digital tools. All digital media, they postulate, build on older media and rework them. They define remediation as "formal logic by which new media refashion prior media forms" (p. 273). This is to say that older forms of communication are reworked in new media, where they take on new characteristics and require new competencies.

Immediacy of access in digital media is unprecedented. Communication transcends physical copresence and geographical borders, rendering the category of interlocutor moot. Furthermore, in a community such as YouTube, where several million people participate in posting, viewing, and communicating synchronously and asynchronously in multiple languages, how do we define audience and speaker? These roles have changed, and so have the competencies they demand.

In social media environments, such as Facebook or YouTube, various modalities and modes are employed to create a rich and immersive experience with digital media. The multiplication of communicative channels raises the question: What makes an effective communicator in these new environments? Communicative competence in digital media extends to multiple modalities and media. For instance, understanding how to create and share a personal video or when to *like* a comment or engage in *tagging* becomes part and parcel of the digital communicative competence repertoire.

Complex relationships in remediated texts affect communication in profound ways. The new mechanism of communication in such texts can be best described as *intermedial flows of meaning*: As old and new media come together and are remediated in each other, fusing and connecting via different modalities and modes, new points of contact are created, and new opportunities for meaning to be produced arise. Meanings flow within and between different modalities of communication: the materialities of communication, our perceptions, its spatial and temporal characteristics, and the meanings inscribed (Elleström, 2011).

Figure 1 provides an example of a video blog posted on YouTube. The flow of meaning in the video blog created by YouTube user geriatric1927 occurs among different material modalities: through the visual, tone of voice, background music, movements of the speaker, interface of the website, and textual comments provided by the users of the website. Meanings also flow between space and time: from the physical space of the room where the video was recorded, to the virtual space of YouTube, to the copresent space-time which is created when the video is viewed. Larger social contexts impact meaning making through this video: the videoblogging conventions established in YouTube, the broader discourses

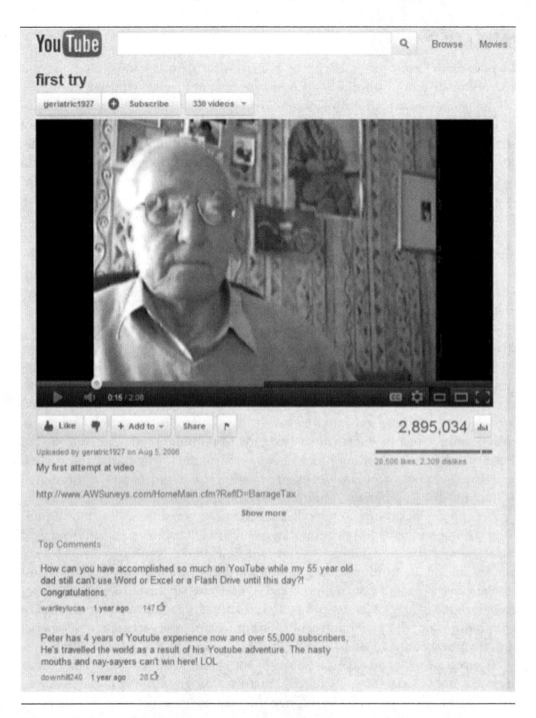

Figure 1. First Try by geriatric1927

of social media use (e.g., the popular belief that social media is a tool of the younger generation), and popular culture (background music as a reference to a particular time period).

VIDEO IN THE REMEDIATED ELT CLASSROOM

The traditional four language skills of print culture—listening, speaking, reading, and writing—provide an inadequate descriptive frame for the forms of communication we can produce today. This statement, though, may be interpreted as politically radical by many, for instance, those who understand the evolution of novel spelling conventions in txting (i.e., text messaging), which evolved to fit the small screens of mobile devices and the time demands of real-time conversation, as lacking in legitimacy by failing to meet established norms and standards. As Carrington (2005) remarks, "txting is clearly constructed in direct opposition to legitimate language" (p. 168). The legitimacy of novel orthographic forms, such as txting, is popularly seen as an affront to the authoritative language in books. However, this resistant stance does not turn back the digital clock. We have new forms of communication, no matter how they are interpreted socially and politically. We cannot ignore them in the classroom.

Carrington (2005) goes on to conclude, "Whatever else txt may be and what it may represent to various sections of our community, it remains an emergent form of text with quite explicit skills, social practices and knowledges associated with it" (p. 171). So what are the new basics in language and literacy education, and what communicative competencies do they require? According to Lotherington and Sinitskaya Ronda (2012), the new basics in language and literacy education must account for the following:

- multiple modes of representation and expression

- multiple mediating technologies and platforms

- connectivity and participatory culture

- collaboration and shared authorship

- dynamic and hybrid texts

- social networking

Tying these new language and literacy basics into the educational understanding of a video requires rethinking what *video* means. The term has been applied to productions of varied lengths and degrees of professionalism from YouTube, which consists largely of short home movies uploaded to a public viewing site, to full-length feature films. Video projection has become fundamental in the digital classroom, where interactive whiteboards are supplanting the static blackboard, and multimedia slide shows created with proprietary software, such as PowerPoint or Keynote, or web-based programs, such as Prezi, have become regular teaching media.

In video sharing sites, such as YouTube and Vimeo, video presentations are uploaded into a multimedia environment where a comments section enables public commentary. Videos as componential in communication are increasingly managed on portable devices with individual screens, such as smartphones. This portability affects the learning space and the learner's agency in that the learner can capture and upload content for analysis and discussion in the language classroom (cf. Bo-Kristensen & Meyer, 2008).

In the following sections, we discuss two case studies of students learning English in different schools in Toronto, Canada: an elementary school and a high school, both in urban areas of high linguistic diversity. The learners in these classrooms were using video in very different ways, putting these new language and literacy basics into contemporary communicative English language learning. The teachers we worked with were well educated, experienced, and keen to be actively involved in research about new ways of teaching language and literacy in the classroom. The research designs include a case study, whereby the researcher designed and conducted an intervention in the classroom in coordination with the class teacher (Grade 11), and an action research project, during which teachers worked together in collaboration with researchers to design an intervention for their own classes (for details, see Lotherington, 2011).

Just Ella: A Multimodal Beauty Project

At Joyce Public School,[1] in northwest Toronto, a cohort of Grade 4–5 students, many of whom have specific learning challenges in addition to being learners of English, explored the notion of beauty using a variety of semiotic resources across multiple media, including small and large video screens. The source text for their explorations was a contemporary feminist reworking of the traditional fairy tale *Cinderella* called *Just Ella*, by Margaret Peterson Haddix (1999).

The beauty project was one of three class projects in 2010–2011. These class projects are developed annually to unite teachers and researchers in the mutual aim of developing exploratory multiliteracies pedagogies that bring the teaching of language (i.e., English and other languages) and literacy (including digital literacies) into the 21st century (see Lotherington, 2011). Our modus operandi is collaborative action research, and our theory–practice discussions constitute in-house professional development. What our learning community strives for is to teach "outside of the box."

Rhea Perreira-Foyle was the teacher who spearheaded this collaborative multimedia project in 2010–2011. Rhea is an experienced, creative teacher-researcher, and she describes her pedagogy as helping children to discover. She explains that

---

[1] With specific permission from the Toronto District School Board, Joyce Public School, and individual teachers, real names are used. The children remain anonymous.

there is no point in identifying children who are ELLs at Joyce Public School because the majority of children are either new immigrants or were born to parents who are, and thus are in some stage of learning English. Complicating their variable exposure to and experience with English is that many also have identified learning challenges. These children must overcome many obstacles to be able to communicate in English in ways that are recognized positively in formal education settings.

Rhea explained that linguistic inclusion is a normal part of inclusive education; English language learning is always integrated into her curricular agenda. Linguistic heterogeneity is the classroom norm in a densely multicultural urban area such as Toronto. In this school board, there are diminishing funds for specialist help with children identified as learning English as a second language (ESL), and given funding challenges and classroom norms, few children are actually designated for specialized ESL assistance. All classroom teachers in Toronto, therefore, are teachers of English.

Including the multiple home languages of the children in classroom learning activities is an ongoing aim of the learning community research agenda. Children bring their home languages into the learning context in ways that assist them educationally and socially. English language acquisition is thus ecologically supported as a language in their growing repertoire that can lean on other proficiencies. In the process, they are experiencing and appreciating the linguistic wealth of their classmates. The approach is consistent with what García (2009) describes as dynamic bilingual education (p. 118): polydirectional language learning. The only language that will be tested, however, is English.

In terms of measurable English literacy, Rhea explained that there is no ideal model. Gifted children, as well as those with challenges, may have difficulty with formal reading and writing in English, but she finds that there is always an area in which each child shines, and she seeks out children's strong communication skills to augment and support their English language learning, embedding writing within multimodal communication. She noted that oral language may be a strength for some children, but it is not valued in the curriculum. This is an interesting observation, indicating that what schools often think of as English language learning is more accurately described as language-specific print literacy. This is verified in the mandatory provincial English (or, alternatively, French) literacy and numeracy tests all students take at Grades 3 and 6, which use text-based literate activities to track punctuation, grammatical accuracy, and limited comprehension and production.[2]

Rhea promotes creative thinking and collaborative learning, encouraging children to help each other. The distributed learning model she uses is fundamental to team-based multimodal production. She scaffolds the mode of inspiration to the children—whether music, art, or movement—to motivate, capture, or

---

[2] Refer to www.eqao.com/Parents/parents.aspx?Lang=E for examples of past tests.

respond to English text. In the beauty project, children were experimenting with multiple senses in different classes, exploring what tasted, smelled, felt, looked, or sounded beautiful to them. Children thus heard beauty as well as saw it in their own ways, alongside more conventional social ideas of beauty. Rhea explained, "They learn not to follow but to develop a love of learning."

The beauty project attracted three other classroom teachers across Grades 4 and 5, and at other grade levels, rendering it cross-age as well as cross-disciplinary. Teaching goals for the group included multimedia communication and multi-sensory engagement to experience beauty. Each teacher focused on a different sense. Rhea concentrated on sound; Andrew, taste; Chris, smell; and Ashleigh, touch. The teachers created different textual products, including stories, music videos, and art, providing students with a cooperative agenda geared towards consolidating multimedia expression.

Rhea began on the Internet, finding sounds that she could play to children for their reactions and to stimulate discussion, asking questions such as "How does a siren make you feel?" She then moved on to music from a range of cultural backgrounds that related to children's home backgrounds (e.g., Jamaican reggae, Chinese opera, Indian and Vietnamese music) to which the children drew in freeform response. Interestingly, Rhea explained that children who are understood to be unproblematic learners often have difficulties with this task because it has no borders; there is no model to emulate. However, the children who have limits and challenges in English writing take this on with abandon, giving flight to their imaginations. This observation begs the question: Where does the teacher draw the line between scaffolding an activity to enable student expression and tethering production to established models, thereby risking shutting down creative expression in favor of precise duplication?

Rhea's use of video in this project was unconventional; the screen was a technical medium for the expression and archiving of multisensory communication and multimodal learning. Following the freeform drawing task, the children extended their musical response by making shadow art on the SMART Board with moving flashlights covered in coloured cellophane. This activity was videotaped, creating a nonverbal musical video. This was a distinctive idea for creating a source for written description that allowed children to mine their own experience and creativity within a collage of multisensory reactions to beauty. The execution of these individually produced but collectively created animations was dependent on the use of English as the language of instruction, and it owed its inspiration to the study of a text-based narrative in English, but it was not a test of grammatical production. Rather, the children's video production was a link in the narrative flow of the project, bringing together diverse media in 3D time-sensitive capture.

What communicative competencies did this multimedia video activity illustrate? It is here that we are faced with the shortfalls of a theory of communicative competence developed for outdated media. In a multimodal project such as this, how is speech to be distinguished and separated from writing? Where is multimodal design—critical to textual creation—accommodated in the communicative framework? How are distributed cognition and shared authorship to be understood in a framework that separates skills, understands media of communication as strictly oral and written, and is only capable of assigning individual authorship to static text?

Instructive to TESOL practice, this project showed how teachers can reconfigure "texts" as multimodal by including multimedia design factors, look at authorship as collaborative and interactive, and redistribute cognition to the collective to support learners who may struggle individually. In this project, the screen was a technical medium that invited a variety of modes of communication, including sound, colour, movement, and narrative text. Aside from relating to each other, these modes related to classroom discourse, including the teacher's instructions and the contributions of other children in the classroom, and to textual products, such as the initial novel read by students and their final projects, which juxtaposed written descriptions and video.

With an updated understanding of communicative competence, teachers like Rhea are willing and able to take calculated, theoretically driven pedagogical risks, giving children (who are understood as being at risk in the school system due to their numerous challenges with English reading and writing) a degree of control over their participation and learning trajectories. This is *agentive learning*: The learner takes agency over his or her progress. The video segment described earlier was combined with other communication media, which were programmed using Smart Notebook, linked to the SMART Board (see Figure 2). Children's finished projects—art projects with bilingual descriptions—were captured in video profiles of the children's multisensory, multimedia journey. These were captured alongside children's narrations in remixes of their project. Using multiple modes of expression to stimulate and envelop English language reading and writing is easy to scaffold, yet rare in the paper-and-pencil world of the ELT classroom.

The beauty project, stimulated by a postmodern retelling of a traditional narrative, exemplifies how children learning English can work through

- multiple modes of representation and expression;

- multiple mediating technologies and platforms; and

- collaboration and shared authorship.

These are fundamentals in a contemporary definition of communicative competence that attends to intermedial flows of meaning.

Mike Myers Public: Remediating Educational Video on Facebook

The second project took place in a high school English classroom in which a group of Grade 11 students participated in learning with Facebook. The 47 participating teens were linguistically and culturally diverse; many were first-generation immigrants, and the majority spoke non-English native languages such as Arabic,

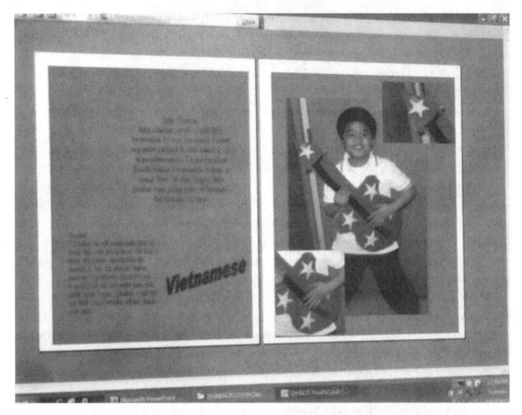

Figure 2. Child's Digital Portfolio of Individually Meaningful Beauty, Bilingually Described

Tamil, Urdu, Sinhalese, Chinese, Swahili, Hindi, and Ukrainian, to name a few. The school, Mike Myers Public, was located in urban Toronto.[3]

For the purposes of this research, a digital application was built on Facebook. My Writing Circle featured three digital environments: a writing environment, a video sharing environment, and a collaborative wiki environment. This section focuses on the video environment which allowed students to post videos from YouTube, add verbal descriptions and tags, and post comments. The video environment was used during the novel study of *Their Eyes Were Watching God,* by Zora Neale Hurston (1937/1998). The novel features a Black female protagonist and explores questions of race, civil rights, gender roles, and the power of language. The students posted videos which provided contextual background to the novel, including themes such as the U.S. Civil War, the Harlem Renaissance, Jim Crow, and the biography of the author.

The application offered students a platform to explore digital communication by engaging with meaning-making through multimedia, utilizing grassroots

---

[3] All names, both in the text and in digital artifacts produced by students, are pseudonyms.

community-produced media for educational purposes, and collaborating digitally. These competencies, as discussed throughout this chapter, are essential in today's digital environments. The experiences that these students created while using the application illustrate how social media can be integrated into formal educational contexts. The use of multimedia texts in an English language classroom highlights the relevance of new communicative competences in language-learning contexts. By expanding the repertoire of educational texts through the inclusion of videos available on YouTube, multilingual and multicultural students gained opportunities to draw on a wider pool of resources in order to make meaningful connections to the powerful English literacies they were acquiring in the classroom. Moreover, learners whose reading and writing in English may just have been developing received opportunities to express themselves via other media and modalities, thereby expanding their expressive repertoire and immersing themselves in the complexities of contemporary communication.

The participating students had a mixed level of experience with social media. In the interviews with participants about their use of digital technologies socially and educationally, a number reported that they used social media, such as YouTube, Facebook, MSN Messenger, and Twitter, for entertainment on a regular basis. It was also not uncommon for these teens to report using new media for utilitarian purposes; for instance, YouTube was mentioned as a great resource for fostering a connection to the global community of believers through access to recorded recitations of religious texts, and Facebook was used to seek homework help from friends.

The use of social media for educational purposes was not a familiar paradigm to these teens. Although the teacher regularly showed YouTube videos in the English class in which the study was taking place, and a class blog was an integral part of the curriculum, students had limited experience with making meaning using social media. They spoke of cautious attitudes towards social media, including Wikipedia and YouTube, as a source of appropriate educational content. Some students even spoke of being discouraged from using Google, a popular search engine, though they could not quite put into words the reasons for having to avoid it.

In responding to the assignment, students had an opportunity to engage with contemporary media culture and to tap into the potential of community-produced media to support their learning. Importantly, by posting videos to the learning application and explaining the relevance of their choices, the students had an opportunity to share their learning and their growing understanding with their peers. The students posted a variety of videos that engaged with the historical context of Hurston's novel in different ways. Several students tagged their videos. A large number of videos were excerpts from documentaries, PowerPoint presentations, or talks related to the topics assigned. A few notable exceptions ventured outside of the traditional style of educational video and posted artefacts of popular culture, or lesser known digital artefacts such as a battle reenactment video, to the My Writing Circle application. Three such examples are examined to discuss multimedia meaning-making, collaboration, and intermedial flows of meaning.

In the first example (see Figure 3), Emma, an academically driven student who opted out of using Facebook socially because it did not provide her with any benefits, submitted an excerpt from a documentary on Zora Neale Hurston. In a veritable example of remediation, it was the old media that were remediated in the new; YouTube, a participatory platform, was used to host a traditional documentary. Although the potential for new ways to communicate were possible through commenting open to global users, the creator of the original video posting chose to ignore these possibilities by disabling the commenting function. It is noteworthy that several students mentioned the instructional nature of videos as a sign of quality. One student highlighted that the videos that were excerpts from documentaries were more valuable for their learning than were the community-produced videos.

A different kind of video was submitted by Alia, a student who described her engagement with different digital media, including Facebook, YouTube, and Twitter. In her submission (see Figure 4) Alia taps into popular culture and tries to make a meaningful connection to the historical context of the Harlem Renaissance, submitting a rap song exploring contemporary issues of racial politics in

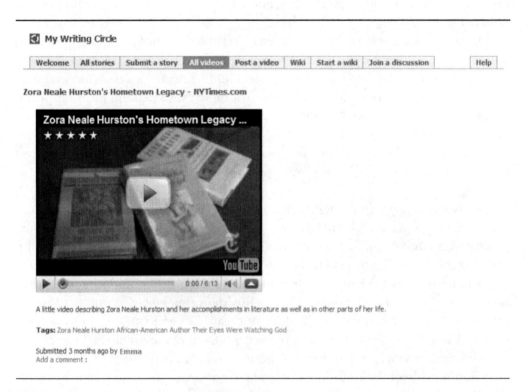

Figure 3. Emma's Documentary on Zora Neale Hurston

My Writing Circle

| Welcome | All stories | Submit a story | All videos | Post a video | Wiki | Start a wiki | Join a discussion | | Help |

Immortal Technique- Harlem Renaissance

04-Immortal Technique Harlem Renaissan..
★ ★ ★ ★ ★

0:00 / 5:27

This is a video, or rather an audio clip, by the rapper named Immortal Technique. In the song he talks about the Harlem Renaissance, and society in general. I found it to be an insightful approach to this topic, that the youth of today could relate to.

Submitted 3 months ago by Alia
Add a comment :

Figure 4. Alia's Rap Song Submission

North America. In this example, the new intermedial flows of meaning are at play; in addition to the image, a musical medium is called upon to engage with meaning-making.

The final example (see Figure 5) is taken from the work of Kamal, a driven and active student who described using Facebook and other social media to seek help from friends with his academic work. In this submission, the video presented a Civil War battle reenactment. The video featured not only footage of the reenactment, but also a background song. Kamal noted this in his written description of the video, stating that the song captured the battle for equal rights. Interestingly, the song playing in the background was *Bonnie Blue Flag*, a song used by the Confederate Army. This intermedial flow of meaning between the visual and the auditory was missed by Kamal; by paying closer attention to the textual dimensions, he misinterpreted the meaning of the song. This example speaks to how the four-skill model is no longer sufficient. In the new digital communicative competence model, all dimensions of meaning-making, including both visual and auditory nonlinguistic cues, become critical. No longer is it possible to rely on words alone to get the full communicative message. Kamal was competent in accessing the textual dimensions of the video (presumably searching for it on YouTube using key words, reading the title of the video, and providing his own textual description). However, the missed ingredients were the clues provided in the video (like the dress of the soldiers) and the background song (associated

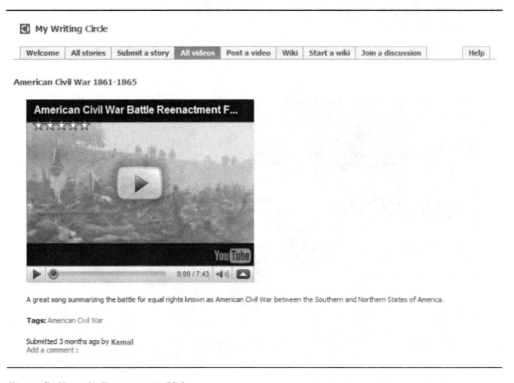

Figure 5. Kamal's Reenactment Video

with the Confederate Army), which rendered Kamal's understanding incomplete and his traditional competence inadequate.

As evident from these examples, different students engaged differently with the meaning-making possibilities of participatory media. Some, like Emma, found the closest possible equivalent to an instructional video. Students' inexperience with using social media to further their learning may have contributed to such cautious use of YouTube. However, Alia's and Kamal's submissions point to some powerful new educational possibilities of digital media: The intermedial flows of meaning between the visual, the verbal, and the musical modalities open avenues for new expression and new learning.

The learning potential of engaging with digital video was also recognized by the students. In their interviews, they spoke about the value of collaborative aspects of video sharing. To them, My Writing Circle provided a platform where digital content could be shared and learning could happen collaboratively. One student admitted to benefiting from resources that others contributed:

> The videos were actually really helpful. Some of the stuff that I had . . . you know how we were given research to find information and post it? It took a long time for me to do it on YouTube, so for someone who is looking for it, you can just click it and it would be there immediately.

Students also recognized that learning through media other than print could be valuable. A student spoke to the experience of using visuals in her learning as the most valuable aspect of using the My Writing Circle application:

> I think I'm going to use more visual in my work. Usually what I use is more writing and stuff, I don't really use . . . I don't usually use visual stuff, even though I like that. I think I'll start using that too. . . . I never really used the videos in my projects or whatever. But I think I want to start doing that. 'Cause it's kind of, it's interesting, it adds a lot of interest to our project.

Although it may be too soon to tell whether these students developed digital communicative competences through using video, it is certain that they approached this experience as a new competence. They mentioned in the interviews how the use of video was a profoundly new paradigm of delivering content to their peers and how they were able to redefine, to a degree, their own learning, which had largely focused on traditional reading and writing abilities. Several of the students said that their experiences with video posting, as well as tagging, were part of their growing competence in using these new media for meaning-making.

The students in the Facebook project were able to engage with the following aspects of digital communicative competence:

- connecting grassroots social media and formal curriculum

- experiencing multimedia meaning-making

- creating a collaborative community of shared learning

REVISITING—AND REMEDIATING— COMMUNICATIVE COMPETENCE

Texts and practices in the new multimedia landscape challenge the limits and the values of 1980s communicative competencies. The demonstrated presence of intermedial flows of meaning suggests a radical rethinking of communicative competence in digital environments. So how can communicative competence be reshaped for digital multimedia environments in the context of the ELT classroom?

First, we need to reconceptualize how the four building blocks of Canale's (1983) description of communicative competence (viz., grammatical, sociolinguistic, discourse, and strategic competence) relate to multimedia environments. Additionally, multimedia communicative competencies are required to scaffold communication in digital environments.

Grammatical competence must extend the formal properties of language encoded alphabetically to a complex suite of media, materials, modalities, and spaces encoded in pixels. Pixelized communication brings with it new ways of encoding and decoding meaning. An array of communicative modes and modalities are combined digitally to create digital bricks that can then be put together in various ways, as exemplified in YouTube videos with commentary or Facebook notes and tagged photos. Grammatical thus branches to multimedia competence—the competence to choose and use a medium or suite of media that maximizes communication. The ruler by which grammatical competence is measured must also be tweaked: from being concerned solely with *correctness* relative to fixed alphabetic standards and static text to also including *creativity* for customizable, dynamic, multimedia texts.

Sociolinguistic competence is expanded by the explosion of online social literacies and digital genres merging modes of expression and inviting inter-locutors from around the world into a shared digital space. The practices of meaning-making are also expanded to include a diverse array of engagements with text and media from anime-inspired fan-fiction[1] to video game–based art; these engagements build identity and community. Sociolinguistic competence recast digitally moves into diverse online-offline contexts of meaning-making which shift with digital currents. This could be viewed as the user's appropriate use of multimedia communication within the technical, social, and multimodal affordances of the context.

New discourse conventions have developed in digital genres and spaces co-created over the past decade, including those encoded in abbreviated orthographies. Rather than debate the correctness of the abbreviated orthographies of texting environments—which is hypocritical in the face of the acceptability of alternative spellings such as *theatre* and *theater* or *colour* and *color* in cultural context—teachers need to rethink spelling in terms of appropriateness to text type. Discourse competences must also expand to take in dynamic, collaborative authorship in digital environments.

Strategic competence requires facility with multimedia that far outstrips the borders of alphabetic language typically taught in the ELT classroom. The teacher must question a much larger panorama of media in the formation of strategies and the conduct of classroom discourse. She or he must consider how the medium or multimedia suite and intermedial processing were planned and conducted and, importantly, whether that was an individual or collegial effort. New discourses are interactive, inviting modding, collegial authorship, and problem solving to build a dynamic customized text. Strategic competence in digital environments moves communication from individual and local to collaborative and global.

This shift from individual to collaborative communication has profound significance in the ELT classroom, where it creates new learning opportunities. Davidson (2011) pioneers a method of collaboration by difference in her

---

[1] Fiction created by fans of a published work or series of works, often without the consent of the author or copyright holder.

undergraduate class which foregrounds student collaboration and autonomy: "Collaboration by difference respects and rewards different forms and levels of expertise, perspective, culture, age, ability, and insight, treating difference not as a deficit but as a point of distinction" (p. 100). Collaboration by difference in an ELT classroom is a fruitful model to encourage the building of bridges across competences, both linguistic and digital.

However, traditional four skills–oriented communicative competencies cannot simply be stretched to describe multimedia environments. The social bases of communication have shifted fundamentally as new technical media invite proliferating new discourses, coding conventions, genres, communities, and identities consistent with the affordances and boundaries of the medium, platform, program, and community created. Reading and writing, once distinguishable, or at least claimed to be, were predicated on static text. Portable technical media, global connectivity, social interactivity, multimodal production, and textual dynamism create the conditions for distributed cognition and collective intelligence; for readers to cowrite, rewrite, or overwrite existing texts; for collaborations between people working asynchronously, even from different parts of the globe; for creative, multimodal expression; and for multilingual inclusion and translation. Unless new multimedia competencies have a place in the classroom, we are teaching the English language as history in preparation for a century that has already passed.

CONCLUSIONS

In the 21st century, we are living in digital culture. The screen does not simply supplement the page; it supersedes it. Our communications are interactive, dynamic, and multimodal. The communicant is now a prosumer; the interlocutor, a digital voice unattached to physical attributes. In this communication landscape, the screen is a primary location for English in varied, complex communicative use, and it is critical to the remediation of a passé conceptualization of communicative competence.

In summary, video in the contemporary ELT classroom is a technical medium for production as well as consumption; a medium that can be analyzed, supported, mixed and augmented by other media, including spoken, recorded, and textual English; and an available medium that forms a part of everyday portable communication devices, such as mobile telephones, handheld games, and MP3 players as well as tablet and laptop computers. These portable screens provide opportunities for agentive English language learning and social participation in English-medium communities, allowing the learner to capture and create language in social context. The learner thus performs language and acquires competence through this performance in conversations, texts, and digital environments. Contemporary digital media incorporate multimodality, so products are not totally language reliant and can interweave and support language with other modes of expression. Digital communication is interactive and collaborative. English language learners can import digital competencies from their social practices in other language communities to support their expressive potential while learning English.

A complex new vision of digital communicative competence is proposed here, which highlights the new challenges involved in theorizing competencies commensurate with the updated definitions of communication in the digital era. Pedagogical implications of this reconceptualization are profound; educators are on the front lines of bringing change to their classrooms. We have described adventurous teachers of English language learners who are collaborating with students and other teachers to invite relevant digital practices and technologies into their classrooms. We invite your participation in the development of exciting, digitally inclusive TESOL pedagogies.

CHAPTER 3

Child Second Language Learners and Videomaking in Three Sites: Opportunities for Developing Multilingual, Multimodal Literacies

Kelleen Toohey and Diane Dagenais

In this chapter, we describe a videomaking project that occurred at three sites of English language learning: a Canadian school enrolling learners from a variety of language backgrounds, a community library in Mexico serving Spanish-speaking children, and a school in northern India enrolling Tibetan-speaking children. We asked children in each site to show what their lives are like. Here, we describe the affordances of videomaking for second language learning as well as some of the constraints associated when schools take on such activities.

Although print literacy has been and will continue to be one of schooling's major goals, the scale and speed of changes that digital technologies have brought to literacy are unprecedented. Many scholars now refer to *multiliteracies*, pointing out that people necessarily make meaning of a wide range of symbolic and representational systems, including language (Coiro, Knobel, Lankshear, & Leu, 2008), but also other media, such as images, music, video, websites, sound, and so on. Stein (2008) argues that schools commonly privilege language (and especially printed language) to represent knowledge, but children use many other media outside classrooms. Many researchers are convinced that teachers must learn how to help children not only critically examine the multimedia messages that surround them, but also design and produce representations that use a blend of language and other media (e.g., Carrington & Marsh, 2005; Coiro et al., 2008; Early & Marshall, 2008; Gee, 2004; Hague & Williamson, 2009; Kress, 2000, 2003; Mills, 2010a, 2010b; Rhodes & Robnolt, 2009; Sanford & Madill, 2008). Hull and Stornaiuolo (2010) argue, "Of course, all children and youth require 21st century tools and practices, and opportunities as well as powerful versions of

We would like to thank the teachers, preservice teachers, and children who participated in this project, and Simon Fraser University for funding this research through a Social Sciences and Humanities Research Council Institutional Grant.

literacy . . . to participate most agentively in their social and economic futures" (p. 85). Interest is growing in the language learning community in how digital and other media might serve as starting points to develop more powerful and engaging literacy learning environments for bilingual and multilingual youth, as evidenced by this volume and the aforementioned studies.

In this chapter, we describe a particular multimodal videomaking literacy activity with three groups of English language learners (ELLs): ELLs enrolled in a Canadian school, Tibetan children learning English enrolled in a boarding school in northern India, and Spanish-speaking learners attending bilingual English and Zapotec[1] lessons at a community library in Mexico. Working with student teachers from Simon Fraser University doing their practica in these sites, we sponsored videomaking projects so that children could show children in the other sites what their lives were like through video. Given our interest in sociocultural theories of learning, we are interested in the affordances and constraints of videomaking for language learning and the physical and social resources, including out-of-school resources, children used in this activity. Generally, our questions are as follows:

1. Does videomaking enable the representation of children's knowledge and practices (bi/multilingual practices in particular) in ways not afforded by typical classroom print and verbal tasks?

2. Does videomaking enhance children's language and literacy learning?

On the basis of the data we have available, our answers to these questions are, of necessity, tentative. Because of distance and the other priorities of those who worked with us, we were unable to collect much more than children's finished projects, exit interviews with the student teachers, and retrospective written reflections from some of them. Nevertheless, we feel the projects were promising and provocative, and they have sparked our continued interest in the activity and in more recent undertakings. Before describing the projects, we briefly review background theoretical and empirical literature that has informed our work. We then describe the process of making the videos, the products children created, and some of the observations we made about children's engagement in the project. We conclude with provisional answers to our two questions and thoughts on how the practice of videomaking may provide important opportunities for language and literacy learning.

---

[1] Zapotec is an indigenous language of southern Mexico, and it is the ancestral language of many of the children who visit the community library.

PREVIOUS LITERATURE

These projects, like our other work, were undertaken from a broadly socio-cultural perspective on learning, in which learning is seen as a social process that engages culturally and historically situated participants in culturally valued activities. Through participation, then, learners develop the kinds of thought and behavior required for taking part in these activities (Rogoff, 2003; Wertsch, 1998). Like many others, we pay careful attention to the social practices of learners in their diverse environments and to the qualities of the physical, social, and symbolic tools available to learners (Dagenais, 2008; Dagenais, Armand, Maraillet, & Walsh, 2008; Lantolf, 2006, 2007; Lantolf & Thorne, 2006; Smythe & Toohey, 2009a, 2009b; Swain, 2005; Toohey, 2000). In videomaking, the physical tools and symbolic tools provided for children are different from those typically provided in schools, and we have been interested in observing how the use of these tools might have effects on social practices in the contexts in which learners are placed.

Another insight of sociocultural theory is that social practices are enacted in different ways in different environments with different tools. From this perspective, the social practice of literacy is a "repertoire of changing practices for communicating purposely in multiple social and cultural contexts" (Mills, 2010b, p. 247). Literacy learning does not refer to the acquisition of a particular skill or a set of skills acquired by individuals and thereafter universally applicable, but rather to sets of practices that take place in particular environments, for different reasons, using varying tools, and involving varying persons, texts, and social relations (Barton & Hamilton, 1998; Gee, 2004; Street, 1984, 1995, 1998). From this perspective, it is a mistake to conceive of literacy as a singular skill; rather, such a view encourages the use of the term *literacies* or *multiliteracies* to refer to the multiple ways humans make sense of sign systems. The multiliteracies literature calls for an expansion of literacy pedagogy beyond linguistic and textual communication to include other forms of expression such as audio, visual, gestural, and spatial modes. Researchers have suggested that a broader approach to literacy education might better reflect the diversity of practices adopted in contexts of emerging communication technologies and respond to the needs of increasingly heterogeneous populations.

Literacy practices at school only occasionally involve the use of new communication technologies and seem firmly centered on particular kinds of print literacy. Several researchers have shown how school literacy practices are sometimes in direct contrast with community practices and argue that literacy researchers should document community literacy practices so as to build on children's outside-school competencies *in* school (Heath, 1983; Heath & McLaughlin, 1993; Hull & Nelson, 2005; Marsh, 2006; Pahl & Rowsell, 2006; Purcell-Gates, Jacobson, & Degener, 2004). "The practices [students] bring to student life from other domains of their lives" (Edwards, Ivanič, & Mannion, 2009, p. 483) are seen as logical and respectful starting places for educational instruction to begin. This imperative has special relevance for second language (L2) learners, with research showing that when such learners are able to maintain ties with their home languages and cultures, they are better able to benefit from school instruction; that is, their school achievement is higher and they demonstrate higher self-esteem and have higher educational and occupational aspirations (Cummins, 2009; Portes & Rumbaut, 2001). This research underlies our first research question: Does videomaking enable the representation of children's knowledge and practices (bi/multilingual practices in particular) in ways not afforded by typical classroom print and verbal tasks?

Although there is research examining the teaching of multimodal literacies more generally to ELLs, only a few studies have specifically focused on videomaking with these learners (Li & McComb, 2011). Very little research is available on videomaking and language learning, and there is little in the literature that analyzes what students learn in videomaking and how this learning is manifested in their completed video projects. We can only speculate about answers to our second question: Does videomaking enhance children's language and literacy learning? Nevertheless, we next describe the videomaking process and some of the video products to illustrate how this activity may support language learning.

THE PROCESS

Toohey had been involved in previous videomaking projects with child second language learners and been impressed by the opportunities the activity appeared to provide for learners to enhance their spoken and written language skills (through activities such as script writing, storyboarding, and oral rehearsal). Also, videomaking seemed to permit and even encourage children to make use of their community language resources and repertoires. In the several "video camps" Toohey sponsored, children were enthusiastic about learning the technical aspects of videomaking and were highly engaged in completing L2 print literacy activities in order to produce the videos. Dagenais had worked with child second language learners on projects in which they gathered and examined visual evidence of multilingual practices in their communities in photos, videos, and material artifacts such as food wrapping. These activities led bilingual and multilingual children to display their competencies in a range of languages and share knowledge of community-based cultural practices that were rarely discussed in their classrooms.

Preservice teacher education students at our university have the opportunity to complete one of their practica in a variety of international sites, including India and Mexico. Building on the basis of the previous video camps, Toohey sponsored an exchange of videos in 2009 with Punjabi-speaking ELLs in Canada and Tibetan-speaking ELLs in India. In 2010, we extended the video exchange to Mexico. We asked the three groups of student teachers to help the children in their practicum sites make a short video about what their lives are like to be presented to children in the other locations.

We had time only to provide a short tutorial ranging from 1 to 2 days in camera functioning and video editing before the preservice teachers' departure to Mexico or India or their placement in Canadian schools. None had received formal training in film production, photographic composition, or professional development in strategies for teaching with this technology as part of their teacher education at that time. In the brief orientation we provided, they were introduced to planning, shooting, and editing video and shown snippets of previously produced children's videos (from the video camps). The video camp videos were multilingual, with children portraying their schools in a variety of languages. The preservice teachers were provided with video cameras, tripods, and MacBooks with the video editing software iMovie installed (we found version 6.0.3 easier to navigate than more current versions) before leaving the university to go on their practica.

THE PRODUCTS

The Canadian Videos

In the Canadian case, four videos were produced by 12 children between 11 and 14 years of age who spoke a variety of languages in their homes. Those children for whom English was not their home language were no longer receiving specialist English as an additional language support in school, but some still struggled with aspects of English, particularly school literacy activities. The preservice teachers who worked with them began the videomaking activity with some basic instruction on using the cameras and, later, editing the footage. With some guidance from the preservice teachers, therefore, the children were able to film and edit their footage on their own to complete 3- to 5-minute videos.

We describe in detail here only one of the videos, but outline each of the four. The first video was titled "Our Passions," and it showed four girls in succession, who introduced themselves and the activities about which they were passionate. The first girl introduced herself and went on to demonstrate hip hop dancing; the second girl described her love of yoga, and the video showed her doing yoga poses; the third and fourth girls were interested in ballet and showed themselves dancing together. The second video, "Lilian's Bad Day," using few words, showed a girl waking up late and subsequently having a terrible day at school. The third video, "Supercalifragilisticexpialidocious," showed four boys and their outdoor activities: riding mountain bikes, snowboarding, and playing soccer.

The fourth video, "Dancing Machine," opened with a pan shot of the students' school with a narrator voiceover: "This is HW School, and one of my friends, named Jenny, is going to be dancing inside." The camera, handheld, then moves from outside the school to a classroom, with the voiceover saying, "Let's go to find

Jenny." Inside a classroom, we see Jenny in ballet shoes dancing while an older girl is clapping and counting as backdrop to Jenny's dancing. When the camera focuses on the older girl, the narrator says, "She's Jenny's teacher. Let's say hello to her." The camera zooms in to a medium shot, and the teacher curtsies and says, "Hi." The narrator asks, "What are you doing?" and the teacher replies, "I'm teaching Jenny." Then the camera focuses on Jenny, who dances for about 20 seconds. The teacher announces she is going for dinner and Jenny should rest, and the teacher leaves. Then text appears on screen: "Even when the teacher had left for dinner, Jenny still practices for her performance." Then we again see Jenny dancing. The teacher reappears and praises Jenny. Jenny says "Thank you" and then dances some more. The scene changes (as do the actors' costumes), and the teacher announces she is leaving for the weekend before leaving the classroom. More text appears on screen: "The teacher had left and the studio wasn't available anymore, yet Jenny found a place to practice more." After this, we see Jenny performing a more contemporary style of dance in a school hallway, with some contemporary music in the background. She completes her dancing, puts on outdoor shoes, and walks out the door of the school. As she walks down the sidewalk in front of the school, off-screen voices say in unison, "Good luck, Jenny. We care for your passion," and the video ends with outtakes the girls have labeled "N.G. Clips Here" (N.G., presumably, is "not good"). We see clips where Jenny falls or one of the students messes up a line. After several of these, the credits appear and the video ends.

The Indian Videos

The 15 Tibetan children who participated in the videomaking exercise were in Classes (Grades) 5 to 7 and were 10 to 13 years old. Their schooling up to Class 5 had been exclusively in Tibetan, and the children were thus fluent readers, writers, and speakers of Tibetan. Starting English instruction in Class 5, but living in a community that received many English-speaking tourists, these children had a range of proficiency in English, with some having rudimentary proficiency to others being quite fluent. The preservice teachers they worked with gave them instruction after school in how to operate the videomaking equipment, and the children did all the filming as well as the planning and scriptwriting. The children were not able to complete the editing of their video before the preservice teachers returned to Canada, so only 3 minutes of the 23-minute raw footage was edited. We first describe here the 3 minutes of edited video and then shift to the raw footage to complete our description.

Unlike with the other videos, the Tibetan children had written a one-page prose outline of the story they intended to tell. From the opening lines of the story, we learn the video concerns "a Tibetan girl from a poor family" whose name is Dolker. No video title announces this, but rather the story begins with a narrator introducing herself and then introducing the characters in the video: Dolker, her three friends, and a "Music Master" (which we understood to mean a music teacher). A title appears next: "Dolker's grandmother: The movie." Then the camera pans the hostel where Dolker lives and (handheld) follows the narrator walking upstairs to the dormitory. Before showing Dolker, wearing traditional Tibetan dress, sitting on her bed and looking at a book, the camera pans the dormitory room showing butter lamps and zooms in on a picture of His Holiness the Dalai Lama on a shelf in the girls' room. Then the narrator tells us, "Every day she was learning and studying, and she was very poor, and she was thinking to help her old grandmother." Dolker's friends burst into her room and ask her (in English) to go outside to play, but she demurs, saying she has to study. The narrator then reappears and tells viewers, "One day she gets some very bad news. Her grandmother got a very serious disease. Hearing this bad news, she cry [*sic*] a lot." Then we see a tight shot of Dolker crying on her bunk bed. The narrator and the camera then take us to "the old age house," focusing on a sign that says "Old Peoples' Home" in English, Tibetan, and Hindi. Next we see Dolker seated beside her grandmother, who is lying in bed while Dolker strokes her arm and back gently. The camera gets a tight shot of the old woman's face. The scene shifts to Dolker again on her bunk bed crying until two of her friends burst in and tell her to get medicine for her grandmother from the School Health Centre. The next scene shows the Centre sign, and Dolker enters, telling the girl in Tibetan traditional dress behind the counter that her grandmother is sick. The cashier tells her to choose a medicine; she selects one, gives the cashier her money, and the cashier says, "It is not enough."

At this point, the edited movie ends; the remainder of our description is based on the raw footage. The next shot shows Dolker asking the Music Master if she can join his music group to learn to sing, and he agrees. Dolker is next shown wandering around the school grounds singing in Tibetan quietly to herself and then singing with a very clear and synchronized voiceover. Then the narrator's voice tells us over a shot of the sign (student-produced): "Then one day she saw a sign" (see Figure 1).

The video then takes us (imaginatively) to Delhi, with the narrator telling us we are in Delhi over a shot of the school gates. Several different shots are taken of the place where the competition is to be held, and then various groups of children perform dances and songs on a stage (e.g., one group of girls dances and sings a Bollywood song). Dolker in fancy-dress Tibetan attire performs on the stage, again with a synchronized voiceover of a Tibetan song. Predictably, first prize goes to Dolker, and she is happy to receive the prize money, but before she arrives back in her hostel, the Music Master tells her that her grandmother has died. The story concludes with Dolker telling the school headmaster that she will donate her prize money "to the poor students at the school." The video ends with individual shots of the actors, who are asked various questions by an off-camera voice. One of the actors who plays Dolker's friend is asked, "Why did you put the old age home in the video?" and she replies, "Because we have to show how we respect our olders [*sic*]."

Figure 1. Sign Shown in Tibetan Children's Video

The Mexican Video

Ten Spanish-speaking children between 8 and 12 years old who were enrolled in local public Spanish language schools participated in the project. The videomaking activities were offered after school in a community library where the children also received bilingual second language instruction in English and Zapotec. The children were all beginning-level ELLs. Their parents did not want them to operate the video cameras for fear that they might break them, so the Canadian preservice teachers did all the filming and editing of the videos. Nevertheless, the children worked closely with three Mexican preservice teachers who were partnered with five Canadian preservice teachers on this project. With guidance from the Mexican preservice teachers, the children decided what to film, identified filming locations, and wrote and rehearsed their scripts. As a group, they produced a 21-minute video and a 7-minute excerpted version of it. In the long version, each scene opens with a bilingual subtitle. For example, the name of the library appears at the bottom of the first shot, and below is the subtitle "Biblioteca Comunitaria—Community Library." The video features the children in eight different settings in and around the community library. The first 2-minute scene opens with a long shot of the children sitting on a carpet in a circle with some of the Canadian and Mexican preservice teachers in the main room of the library. The children are drawing in notebooks while the preservice teachers lean in to

Figure 2. Mexican Children Working on Video Scripts

observe them, talk with them, and look at their drawings. Close-up shots show the children's drawings that illustrate objects with English words written underneath. We can hear laughter and a combination of Spanish and English spoken by the children and student teachers.

The following shots show the children and preservice teachers playing a warm-up game on the carpet. The next short shots show two Mexican preservice teachers taking turns to show and read the children's illustrations and writings. For example, one preservice teacher reads, "I like chocolate cake." Close-up shots focus on the children's work. In the second scene, which lasts about 8 minutes, each child takes a turn sitting facing the camera. Some speak English and others speak Spanish to say their name, where they live, their age, and the names of members of their family. Some children show a picture of their family as they talk, and others refer to or read a printed script. The parts of the video during which they speak Spanish are subtitled in English.

The third scene opens with a long shot of a multicolored mural that spans a wall along a side street near the community library and zooms in on two boys who explain that the mural announces upcoming parades planned for the Day of the Dead. In this clip, which lasts 11 seconds, the boys improvise a description in Spanish (with English subtitles) of the way this holiday is celebrated in their community and in their families. The fourth scene lasts about 2 minutes and is composed of several clips of three girls who lead a guided tour in English outside of the local school, followed by clips that show all the children playing basketball in the school playground.

The fifth scene is roughly 3 minutes long and features a guided tour of the local Catholic church led by three boys in English and then Spanish. In the first clip they tour the inside of the church, in the next one they introduce the priest, and the last one features the bell ringer, who is ringing the bell in the church tower. The sixth scene lasts about 4 minutes and shows three girls standing under a large tree on the university sports field a few blocks away from the community library. The camera pans the playground and the surrounding mountains and then zooms in as the girls speak English to talk about the view of the mountains and the sports practiced on the field. The next clip includes traditional Mexican mariachi[2] music and features all the children engaging in activities such as races, skipping, and a game of "soccer-baseball" that combines elements of both sports. The seventh scene lasts 40 seconds and features a long shot of the backs of the children and the preservice teachers as they walk back to the community library along a pothole-filled road next to a wall covered in graffiti. The video closes with a minute-long scene that shows the children painting a colorful mural depicting a book tree along the outside wall of the community library.

DISCUSSION

In many ways, it is impossible to compare the three videos. They vary greatly in length, and whereas the Canadian students had time enough to edit their videos and add text and titles to them, the Tibetan children were unable to complete editing and titling their video. The Mexican videos were not shot or edited by the children, but were planned and acted by the children. Whereas the Mexican and Tibetan children's videos contain text and dialogue, the Canadian students' "Lilian's Bad Day," for example, contains very little language in the finished product, but planning it required a great deal of discussion among the videomakers, and it may be that with more time and more instruction, these children could have made more complex and more language-rich productions.

One aspect of the video project was unrealized. We had planned to show the children the videos produced by children in the other sites and to gather data about their reception. Unfortunately, because of time and distance, we were unable to observe the sharing of the videos. In future projects, we will be sure to factor this activity into our plans, because we believe that this might have given us interesting data.

Despite these shortcomings, we think there is sufficient evidence in the videos themselves to begin to address our research questions. With respect to the first question about videomaking enabling children to represent knowledge and practices not afforded by typical classroom tasks, we found it particularly interesting that in many of the videos, the children portrayed activities they engage in outside school. Only one of the Canadian videos ("Lilian's Bad Day") has any-

---

[2] Mariachi is a genre of music that originated in Mexico. Mariachi bands usually include violinists, guitarists, and trumpeters.

Figure 3. Filming the Mexican Children's Video

thing to do with school. The portrayal of children's expertise in dancing, yoga, snowboarding, soccer, singing, mountain biking, and so on is not easily conveyed in print, but the video allows the children to display their interests and talents. In the Mexican video we see the inside of the community library and the exterior of the local school and schoolyard. We are given a tour of the interior of the Catholic church as the children introduce us to Catholic saints, rites, the priest, and the bell ringer. We are shown a large street mural announcing the Day of the Dead while the children explain how this holiday is celebrated. And finally, we are shown the local university sports field that serves as a play area for children and provides a view of the surrounding mountains. The video allows the children to show us some of their out-of-school activities in a way that enables them to use visual representations to complement their oral descriptions and provide a richer account of practices in their community.

In the Tibetan video, we see cultural representations that add to the texture of the story: the butter lamps, the picture of the Dalai Lama, Tibetan dress, and Tibetan songs. Furthermore, the scene of Dolker gently stroking her grandmother and the close-up shots of the old woman's face add immeasurably to the pathos of the story the children tell. None of these representations or details make it into the text of the story the children wrote, a one-page story that reads much like a typical classroom writing task. This video not only contains traditional cultural representation, but also incorporates a familiar global phenomenon: a music contest for which the prize is money.

In short, as evidenced by the children's videos, videomaking seems to enable the representation of children's knowledge and practices in ways that would be difficult to manage in typical classroom tasks. In the Mexican and Indian videos, the children were able to include their bilingual language resources to communicate information and share knowledge of religious and cultural practices adopted in the larger context. As Brass (2008) notes in his videomaking project with bilingual youth in the United States, video facilitates the integration of local knowledge, the recontextualization of cultural information, and the overlap of official and nonofficial learning contexts.

Finally, with respect to all the videos, with only some basic instruction from the preservice teachers in using video cameras and filming techniques, we see the children using filmic techniques they may be familiar with from outside school. They all follow a narrator with a handheld camera; some use tight close-ups for portraying emotion; they pan scenes to give viewers a sense of the surroundings of a scene. Although it is clear that these are novice videomakers and that more instruction and experience would help them improve their videos, we see the children in all cases building on knowledge they probably have not acquired in school and able to represent that knowledge in the video texts they create.

Our second question, about videomaking enhancing children's language and literacy learning, like the first, can only be answered tentatively with the data we have available. If multimodal literacies are understood to include multiple forms of expression in order to make meaning, it follows that teaching multimodal literacies involves showing children that there are multiple means of communicating, beyond language and print alone. We can consider that videomaking offers a more equitable approach to teaching language learners because it enables them to draw on multiple nonlinguistic resources to communicate and allows them to anchor oral information in the visual field to express ideas. During video production, the language learners were able to select these resources according to their needs and their language abilities in order to draw attention, transmit a stimulating message, and position themselves in a powerful way as people who are rich in knowledge.

For example, in an early scene from the Mexican video, the children had the option to present themselves in Spanish or English as they shared visual and oral information about their families, which signaled that using both their first and second languages was a legitimate practice in this language learning context. It also allowed the children to show the viewers that they had achieved a certain level of competence in their language of expression. Also, while speaking to the camera, the children could refer to or read a script, which enabled them to draw on written support while talking. Moreover, by showing a picture of their families and without having to explain in words, the children could quickly share information that would situate them as a member of a social group. That is, the pictures provided visual clues as to their positions in their families and their resemblance to other family members. In addition, the video provided a form of expression in which they used gestures and smiles to communicate their pride and attachment to their families.

In addition, as recorded in our field notes, the retrospective interviews with the preservice teachers, and their written reflections on the videomaking process, the children worked diligently on writing their storyboards and scripts and on practicing their lines. Although we did not measure the children's literacy development in this project, we did observe that the videomaking provided them with added opportunities to make meaning through a variety of modes of expression.

The Canadian video described in detail here shows a rudimentary story arc. The video is mostly a display of Jenny's dance prowess, but the videomakers situate their video in context with outside shots of their school and movement into the school. They introduce a dramatic element—Jenny's persistence in practicing and her friends' support of her dedication to her passion. The text shots were prepared by the students and are grammatically perfect, as is the voiceover script. Because we did not observe the process of their videomaking, we cannot tell whether the girls' language use progressed over the course of the activity, but we can say that the final product displayed competence.

The Tibetan children's video, with the raw footage and the uncompleted final copy, displays dramatically the language learning practice involved in videomaking for these children. They completed a written précis of the script as well as several storyboards with plans for shot types. As seen in their raw footage, the children's repeated attempts to get a satisfactory shot or scene show them practicing lines and, over time, improving their expression. The videomakers found it necessary to incorporate print into their video, with titles and signs they produced and filmed. Although we do not have the process data in this case, the preservice teachers told us in exit interviews that the children had been highly engaged in discussing the video as they made it and in collaborating on ideas to improve it.

We think these videos could have been more productive for language learning and use, but as a first (and no doubt rushed) attempt in which children were learning to use both the camera equipment and the editing program, this production can be seen as a start toward the representation of more complex and enriched meanings. What the children can convey in printed scripts, visuals, music, spoken dialogue, and so on is much richer than what they could convey only in print. For this reason, we think the answer to our second question (Does videomaking enhance children's language and literacy learning?) is a positive "maybe" and one that requires further investigation.

CONCLUSION

Our analyses of data in these projects are suggestive, rather than conclusive, but we are sufficiently encouraged by what we have seen to design projects that might provide more complete information for analysis and to advocate for videomaking as a promising classroom practice for language learning. The children whose videos are described here were engaged in the process, and their enthusiasm for displaying their cultural and linguistic repertoires was obvious. Preparing a product collaboratively that could be presented to others, a product of which the children were proud, was clearly of interest to them, and videomaking allowed them to be more expressive than they might have been if the medium had been limited to print.

Others have pointed out that multimodal projects may be somewhat more difficult to implement in school settings than in other settings. In the Canadian case, the projects were completed in school, whereas the Mexican and Tibetan videos were completed in out-of-school contexts. The time that videomaking takes is extraordinary in "school time"; transitions between subjects take place with regularity in many schools, but videomaking projects take longer than typical class periods, and the disciplines they call on are not easily limited to "mathematics" or "reading" or "science." Also, such projects can be seen as taking time away from what many schools consider the gold standard: print literacy. Although we are not suggesting that print literacy is unimportant in schools, we think that 21st century citizens will have to navigate, make meaning from, and be critical of more than print modalities. Creating products in multiple modalities might be among the best ways students will learn how to understand the messages such products contain.

In closing, we also wish to emphasize that we do not think that multimodal projects like videomaking should be celebrated uncritically. We do not expect beginning-level writers to write good novels (although they might write touching sentences or phrases), and we should not expect novice filmmakers to do their best possible work as beginners. Multimodal tools are as complex as other communication media, and we think that videomaking practices might be returned to again and again in school contexts so that students have the opportunity to refine their skills and make videos that tell compelling stories from the perspectives of those who are too seldom heard from—immigrants and English language learners.

CHAPTER 4

Mediating Identities: Digital Identity Projects in an ESL Classroom

Allyson Eamer and Janette Hughes

This chapter presents a case study that explores the potential of new media and digital literacies to support language learning and acculturation for English language learners (ELLs). Eighteen Toronto middle school ELLs with limited English proficiency and digital literacy used images, music, and narrative in both English and their native language to author digital poems and stories in their classrooms. This project provided the students with a forum to construct, negotiate, and communicate their identities as new Canadians. The use of multimodal forms of expression was particularly beneficial when working with ELLs. The ability of multimodality to overcome the linguistic limitations required to author traditional text-based narratives makes it highly effective for facilitating a sense of autonomy and agency over the language learner's own stories. Multimodality was also seen in this study to enhance the learning of a variety of English language skills, such as vocabulary building and organizing ideas for speaking and writing. The students had emigrated from developing countries with limited access to quality English language education and to information and communication technologies, factors which some research has related to a diminished sense of entitlement to claim legitimacy as a Canadian and as a speaker of English.

This study is an exploration of the factors involved in English language learning, identity negotiation, and digital storytelling. The objective of this research was to conceptualize the relationship between new media and ELLs' creation of personal texts as a means of constructing their identities. The research focuses on this question: How do ELLs use multimodal forms of expression to construct, negotiate, and communicate their identities? In addition to analysing how newcomer preteens would use this school-based opportunity to express their identities through multimodal means, we analysed the students' language learning outcomes and their development of digital literacy skills. In this research project,

---

All images selected by the students, and those presented herein, do not conflict with copyright law, given that they are used in compliance with the fair use exemptions provided to university researchers who use the images for educational purposes. Names of students that appear in this chapter are pseudonyms.

recent immigrant students to Canada, aged 10–13 years, were asked to create a digital text (either a story or a poem) that explored aspects of their lives in their home countries and their lives in Canada. The project positioned ELLs as storytellers of their own personal learning and growth, and offered them opportunities to experience *narrative reconstruction* as they reflected on their lives, their learning, their interests, their past experiences, and their goals for the future (Hull, 2003).

THE URBAN CANADIAN CONTEXT

According to a recent report from Statistics Canada (2005), when Canada celebrates its 150th anniversary in 2017, one out of every five people in Canada will be a visible minority. Toronto, Montreal, and Vancouver are the cities of choice for nearly two-thirds of all immigrants who arrive in Canada (Frideres, 2006), and educators in the urban schools that serve these cities typically find themselves striving to meet the linguistic, social, and educational needs of immigrant students. To this end, every teacher in these settings is an English as a second language (ESL) teacher and has a role in implementing strategies to increase ELLs' sense of belonging, ownership, and relevance with respect to the school culture, the curriculum, and the broader community while also facilitating their acquisition of English.

As immigrants arrive in neighbourhoods populated, at least in part, by people who share their cultural and linguistic heritage, children are increasingly likely to attend schools where their languages are heard in the hallways and on the playgrounds. Although home languages may have moved into public spaces, and cultural artefacts may be welcomed therein, immigrant children are quick to realize that English is the language required for social and academic success. Learning this language while also juggling two sets of cultural expectations and scripts can be challenging and frustrating for an immigrant student.

STUDENT IDENTITY AND
ENGLISH LANGUAGE ACQUISITION

Neighbourhood demographic changes have resulted in increased public awareness of identity politics. Immigrants and native-born Canadians alike are increasingly exposed to census data and demographic projections and to journalistic, scholarly, and best selling texts that focus on how the national identity is being shaped via the coexistence of multiple cultural and linguistic heritages. With the combined and cumulative impact of globalization and transnationalism, it should come as no surprise that current studies are demonstrating that cultural enclaves have developed ethnolinguistic vitality, allowing for a multitude of identities and allegiances within an individual, each of which is shaped by numerous factors such as interlocutors, context, audience, and the desire to achieve social distance or proximity (Giampapa, 2001; Qadeer, 2003; Reitz & Banerjee, 2007; Walks & Bourne, 2006). Identity for individuals and for communities is constructed with reference to group membership boundaries. Because boundaries are increasingly permeable, it can be argued that minority newcomers to Canada and their children are experiencing increased agency in negotiating their own identity claims rather than having identities ascribed to them.

The role of the school in the production and reproduction of cultural norms cannot be overstated with respect to its impact on students who are immigrants or the children of immigrants. Indeed, Morgan (1997) believes that the ESL classroom is a unique site in which language learning and identity construction occur simultaneously. Toohey (2000) is one of many researchers who have studied the role of school in ascribing identities to immigrant students. She demonstrates how identities were "manufactured" by school and classroom practices for each of the students in her study as early as their kindergarten year. She further points out how the inequitable distribution of linguistic resources (e.g., access to oral interactions with peers) limited the opportunities for minority-language students to appropriate classroom language and to speak from positions of power. Toohey goes on to suggest that five interrelated factors are necessary for identity construction: academic competence, physical presentation, behavioral competence, social competence, and language proficiency. Without the linguistic and cultural skills to negotiate their own identities, immigrant students could be at risk of conforming to identities ascribed to them by others.

NARRATIVES

The process of creating a narrative of one's immigration experience is an empowering and complex one, especially for immigrant children who generally have little or no power with regard to the emigration decision (Furman, 2005). For children, constructing the migration story provides agency where none was experienced originally. Furman (2005) underscores that identity is relational, dynamic, fluid, and always under construction. She argues that although the migrant narrative is necessarily one of loss and estrangement, it is also one of possibility, and the migrant has agency in shaping a new hybrid identity. As Hull (2003) points out, "the ability to render one's world as changeable and oneself as an agent able to direct that change is integrally linked to acts of self-representation through writing" (p. 232). Narratives are social artefacts, and "the narrated self is constructed with and responsive to other people" (Miller, 1994, p. 172).

A number of researchers (e.g., Cummins et al., 2005; King & Ganuza, 2005) have analysed students' accounts of their immigration experiences and found that the students exhibited a sense of agency in constructing a dual identity that served their needs in a complex and challenging environment. To understand immigrant identity construction and navigation, researchers have studied narrative in fiction (Cortés-Conde & Boxer, 2002), narrative in personal journals

(Norton Peirce, 1995), and poetry written by immigrants (Kouritzin, 2006). If one accepts that language is "the primary way in which we construct our realities . . . [and] the vehicle through which we ascribe meaning, make sense of our lives, give order to our world and relate our stories" (Anderson, 1997, p. 204), then surely it is incumbent upon all teachers, especially ESL teachers, to provide the means and the tools that allow immigrant students to communicate their stories with their peers, their schools, and their larger communities in spite of limited proficiency in English. The present case study was conducted with the same goal of exploring the narratives and poetry of students in middle school classrooms, but it also allows for multimodal expression in addition to traditional text.

MULTIMODALITIES AND PERFORMANCE

The argument for a pedagogy that takes into account not only traditional print and oral literacies, but also visual and multimodal representations, has been well established in the literature (Cope & Kalantzis, 2000; Cummins, Brown, & Sayers, 2007; Kress, 2003; Kress & Van Leeuwen, 1996; New London Group, 1996). Digital stories have greater potential than oral or print-based stories to enhance the power of narrative for identity negotiation, because they can be "told" with minimal language proficiency and are easily broadcast, creating a stronger sense of audience and performance. Digital media facilitate the convergence of multiple modes of expression which can foster the strengths of diverse learners (i.e., visual, aural, spatial, gestural, and linguistic). For instance, the photograph or image can be a powerful tool in the creation of a digital narrative. In fact, Furman (2005) maintains that images are the basis of all of our stories. She explains that when telling stories of events that have occurred in our lives, we base our narratives on a series of snapshot-like memories we have of a given experience. We attempt to sequence and link the snapshots chronologically and to fill in the gaps between them in order to create a coherent, fully developed narrative. Therefore, digital narratives that explicitly include images may in fact correspond better to students' mental representations of their own stories. Likewise, music can play an important role in the construction of a digital story or poem. The playlists on an adolescent's iPod signal the social, cultural, and linguistic communities with which he or she identifies. Including such personally relevant music in a digital narrative could thus be an excellent way for a student to express his or her identity to peers and teachers.

When students are given opportunities to share their *identity texts* with peers, family, teachers, and the general public through media, they are likely to make gains in self-confidence, self-esteem, and a sense of community belonging through positive feedback (Cummins et al., 2007). When students write and post stories and poetry in digital environments, such as blogs or social networking media like Facebook and YouTube, they place their work more directly on the public stage, moving it beyond an audience of one (i.e., the teacher) and making it accessible to a much larger group of people (Hughes, 2008).

CASE STUDY WITH MIDDLE SCHOOL ELLS

The present research consists of a case study involving 18 middle school ELLs between the ages of 10 and 13 in the Greater Toronto area public school system. The participants attended schools at which more than half of the students spoke a language other than English as their first language. Most of the participants had been in Canada for less than 1 year and originated from South or East Asia. All students were invited to create digital stories or poems in which they could describe themselves with still images, video, music, text, and an audio narration track. Several introductory lessons took place in which discussions and corresponding mini-tasks occurred on the theme of dynamic, multifaceted, and relational identities. Example discussion points included "we are always changing and growing," "we can be a teacher sometimes and a student sometimes," and "we can feel at home in two or more places." ELLs with more advanced English proficiency were also introduced to digital poetry writing to provide opportunities to create links between themselves and their communities. Students were shown sample digital texts based on George Ella Lyon's (n.d.) poem "Where I'm From" and were encouraged to collect images from home and from the Internet to support their own conceptualizations of "where I'm from."

Students found images, video, and music online and collected these artefacts in a folder before piecing them together to support a coherent narrative. Some of the students, particularly those who had been in refugee camps waiting to emigrate, had minimal computer experience. They needed support to learn how to conduct Internet image searches, create folders on a shared network drive, save images, download videos and music, and use Windows Movie Maker or Microsoft Photo Story software. Therefore, a great deal of time was spent providing small-group instruction on basic computer skills. Some students chose to juxtapose elements of their past and current lives, activities, and environments, whereas others chose to focus almost exclusively on their lives in their countries of origin. Students were invited to narrate their stories in English, their first language, or a combination of both. Some students elected to refrain from voiceover narration altogether and used text overlays exclusively. All students were offered assistance with spelling and grammar in the English text that accompanied the images, and some students were able to benefit from the assistance of an Urdu-speaking research assistant.

DATA COLLECTION AND ANALYSIS

The connection between place/displacement and identity frames this work. Therefore the analysis of students' image, video, music, and language choices was done through the theoretical lens of identity negotiation in an effort to learn how each child was integrating or wrestling with multiple, and in some cases conflicting or shifting, affiliations, loyalties, and values. Consistent with the approach taken by Measor and Sikes (1992), the data in the present study were also considered in terms of the selection, presentation, and interpretation of life experiences by the participants. That is, we considered which stories were included by students and which events were omitted, as well as which language(s) were used to describe specific details. Also shaping the present analysis was the theoretical notion that if "our identity is constructed by what we choose to remember, to include, to voice, to make public, then surely, what we choose to forget, to exclude, to keep silent, and private is also key to that identity" (Norquay, 1999, p. 3).

All analysis was qualitative, in keeping with the established practice of in-depth studies of classroom-based learning and case studies in general (Stake, 2000). The data consisted of (a) field notes, (b) students' writing, (c) interviews with students, (d) interviews with teachers, and (e) the digital stories/poems created by students. The analytic methods included thematic coding (Miles, 1994), in which the data were coded for major themes and subthemes across data sources, and the codes were revised and expanded as more themes emerged. Because of the complex blending of multimodal data elements, we also used the digital visual literacy analysis method of developing a "pictorial and textual representation of those elements" (Hull & Katz, 2006, p. 50). That is, we juxtaposed the spoken words from recordings with original written text; the images from digital texts; and data from interviews, field notes, and video recordings to facilitate the "qualitative analysis of patterns" (Hull & Katz, 2006, p. 50).

RESULTS

The digital stories and poems authored by the students in this study constitute what Cummins et al. (2005) refer to as identity texts. Through these texts, the students demonstrated that they were working out their place in the world, a task which was developmentally appropriate given their adolescence and compounded by their juggling of two cultural scripts and two languages. (Samples of the students' work can be found at http://faculty.uoit.ca/eamer/Social_LanguageLearning.html and http://faculty.uoit.ca/hughes/where-i-m-from.html.)

The Cases of Daniel and Mariam

At 13 years old, Daniel was the oldest participant in this study and the only student from China. In Daniel's case, it is clear that his out-of-school multiliteracy interests and activities, in particular his passion for Japanese anime and his technological expertise, comprise a large part of his identity. Adding video was not a requirement of the digital poem assignment, yet Daniel went to great lengths to capture various video clips from the Internet which he then edited using Windows Movie Maker, removing the default soundtrack in order to accommodate his own soundtrack. This kind of digital *remixing*—cobbling pieces of media together into a new text—is a popular practice among many adolescents. As Knobel and Lankshear (2008) remind us, "remix practices are fruitful and rewarding ways of becoming proficient within a range of new literacies" (p. 30). Remixing requires a number of technical and literacy skills throughout the construction process, including making design decisions; working with a storyboard; drawing on visual literacy skills; manipulating sound and images; knowing how to use production tools; and understanding the impact of camera angles, lighting, and transitions. In addition, remixing is a cultural practice that draws on the lived experiences of adolescents. Although he did not wield the digital camera himself, Daniel, a quiet young man who was reluctant to speak openly in class, took images found on the Internet and merged them in a technologically sophisticated way to confidently express himself and his view of the world. Although he was not accustomed to sharing his opinions or his work in class, he created a digital poem that he was thrilled to share with others.

Mariam's case is also noteworthy. Mariam was a quiet student from Afghanistan. She did not speak much in English or in her native Pashto, and she chose to produce her video without a voiceover narrative in either language. Despite having limited computer skills and a shy personality, Mariam produced a compelling digital story that was unique among those of her peers. What was most remarkable about her digital story was that 11 of her 14 images centred on human beings, food, or a combination of the two (e.g., a young girl cooking, a hungry child crying). Only three of her chosen images (i.e., an opulent house, a mountain range, and a picture showing Canadian coins) did not fit this pattern, although it is perhaps worth mentioning that two of those three deal with privilege, power, and consumerism.

When Mariam was asked if she wanted to include a soundtrack for her digital story, she requested a song by Avril Lavigne titled "When You're Gone." Her choice—a departure from those of her friends, all of whom chose songs by Miley Cyrus and Beyoncé—may have been a quiet assertion of independence. By choosing an equally popular artist for her soundtrack, but one that her friends had presumably not considered, Mariam was able to indicate her sociocultural competence in the context of a Canadian school while simultaneously signalling a desire to think for herself.

Major Characteristics of Identity Texts: Heritage Values, Cross-Cultural Appreciation and Variations Between Genders

With the help of an Urdu-speaking research assistant, some students for whom Urdu was a first or second language could communicate their thoughts, both orally and in writing, in Urdu, which could then be translated into English. In these instances, the research assistant would verify with the students that the English translation accurately conveyed their intended message. The use of pronouns and conjunctions in the students' writing was very telling in terms of identity. One student wrote in English, "This is the flag of *my* country." The image of the flag of Pakistan that accompanied the narration signalled the child's firm embracing of her heritage even as she had made a home in a new country. Another child, speaking in Urdu to the research assistant, said of movie star Shahrukh Khan, "He is an actor, *but* he is a Muslim." However, this contrast was absent in the English words he used when independently composing the caption that accompanied the image of Khan. The words (in Urdu) "*but* he is Muslim" signalled this child's exposure to discussions in his native language regarding which behaviours might jeopardize one's claim to be a Muslim. Without an invitation to use multimodalities and their first languages, it is hard to imagine how educators and researchers might glimpse these students' expressions of values that are central to their life experiences.

Soundtrack choices proved quite interesting as well, given that many participants chose songs that were from soundtracks for films (e.g., Indian/Hindi action thriller *Don*), TV shows (e.g., Disney Channel's *Hannah Montana*), Internet videos (e.g., American band My Chemical Romance's *Black Parade* featured in YouTube clips of *Dragonball Z*), or animated films (e.g., Japanese band Aqua Timez's *Beyond a Thousand Nights* from the film *Bleach: Memories of Nobody*). Most remarkable of all is that no student chose a soundtrack song that was sung in his or her native language. This is true even for the non-English songs; the Japanese song was chosen by a Chinese student, and the Indian/Hindi song was chosen by a Pakistani Urdu-speaking student. In both of these cases, the cultural clout of Japanese anime and India's Bollywood in North America would account for the appropriation of these songs by the students. Norton Peirce (1995), who describes the social construction of immigrants as "illegitimate speakers" of English, explains that over time, and with evidence of cultural and linguistic competence, the immigrant could be said to have acquired "legitimate speaker" status with the right and power to "impose reception" (pp. 23–24). It is worth noting that cultural competence for immigrant children in 21st century urban North America may include the ability to recognize characters in Japanese-produced anime and in Indian-produced Bollywood films.

There were also some notable gender differences in the content of the identity texts. Boys' texts tended to focus on male sports heroes and action movie stars from their home countries, whereas girls' narratives focused on female singers and actresses from their home countries, along with their North American counterparts. For boys, migration and continuity was described primarily in terms of the video games, TV shows, or films they viewed in each country. On the other hand, girls referred more to aspects of their immediate surroundings when describing migration and continuity, with comments ranging from "Afghanistan and Canada both have mountains with snow" to "In Canada I have a cat that looks like the one my aunt had at my old house." Both boys and girls included multiple images of food from their homelands, and both juxtaposed human-made landmarks in their home countries with those in Canada (e.g., the Faisal Mosque in Islamabad and the CN Tower in Toronto). Students of both genders included images of the natural beauty of their homelands, along with animals common to their countries of origin.

LEARNING OUTCOMES

Having considered how the image, text, and soundtrack choices related to identity negotiation, we revisited the same choices—this time through the lens of outcome-based language learning and the acquisition of digital literacy skills. Using the Ontario Ministry of Education's (2005, 2008) ESL guides, we were able to assess the extent to which the students' digital projects addressed the learning expectations required for their age and grade levels. In general, these guides require ELLs in Ontario to demonstrate an increasing ability between Grades 4 and 8 to compose text with an awareness of a specific audience. Students are also expected to be able to use graphic images and various forms of text to fit a specific purpose. The participants in the present study clearly met and in some cases exceeded this expectation, because all were able to demonstrate an awareness of communicating with a broad audience for the purpose of sharing their migration stories. We also looked at the standards established by the National Council of Teachers of English (NCTE; 2008) and the International Society for Technology in Education (ISTE; 2012) for the development of digital literacy skills. Specific learning outcomes taken from these guides and standards are presented in the following sections. It should be noted here that it is not the intent of this study to demonstrate *improved* learning outcomes. What will be demonstrated in the following section is rather the effectiveness of these student-produced multimodal migration narratives as authentic means through which students can demonstrate the ability to perform skills required by the provincial curriculum.

Comparing and Contrasting

Ontario ESL standards indicate that ELLs should be able to demonstrate the ability to use the technique of comparing and contrasting to organize their ideas. This skill was highly evident in the juxtapositions featured in the student work shown in Figures 1–4. In all four cases, the images served to scaffold written language production. Zoha, in contrasting plant life native to Pakistan and to Canada, wrote, "It is a jasmine flower. I like its smell. It is a symbol of Pakistan. It is a maple leaf. It looks like a flower. It is a symbol of Canada" (see Figure 1). Atif contrasted the use of public space in both countries: "In Pakistan, I saw a street show with goats and monkeys. In Canada when summer comes people go to park and listen to music which I enjoy as well" (see Figure 2). Mariam presented her

Figure 1. Juxtaposition of Flora by Zoha

Figure 2. Juxtaposition of Public Spaces by Atif

two favourite actresses, a Bollywood star and an American TV star. She did not explain the context in which she deemed Kareena Kapoor, the Bollywood actress, to be her favourite, but presumably she was exposed to this actress while living in Pakistan awaiting emigration to Canada. She wrote, "Kareena Kapoor is my favourite actress." Then, over a photograph of Miley Cyrus, she wrote, "This is my favourite actress in Canada. I like her because she is a good singer" (see Figure 3). Kashif used images and voiceover to juxtapose two films he enjoyed watching: one in Pakistan and one in Canada (see Figure 4). It is interesting that in each of these four cases, the two images being compared and contrasted were ordered according to the country in which the featured person or item was encountered,

Figure 3. Juxtaposition of Celebrities by Mariam

Figure 4. Juxtaposition of Films by Kashif

with the image related to Canada always coming second. Aside from reflecting simple chronology, this may also suggest the establishment of the home country experience as the reference point for all new experiences in Canada.

Although being able to compare and contrast is an important skill, in future iterations of this project we would encourage more students to integrate their observations about their lives and interests both before and after moving to Canada into a narrative. Storytelling that employs the use of different verb tenses, time markers, and rich description would certainly help students develop greater vocabulary skills. However, more sophisticated narration was simply not an option

Figure 5. Sequence of Migration According to Engagement With Specific Media by Abdullah

for many of the students because their English language skills were so limited; most of them were new to Canada and had only a very basic level of English.

Using Sequencing to Organize Writing and Speaking

Ontario ESL standards also include the ability to sequence events within a short original written narrative or oral presentation on a topic of personal knowledge or interest. In the sequence shown in Figure 5, Abdullah established the transition between his first home in Afghanistan, his temporary home in a Pakistan refugee camp, and his current home in Canada by indicating which media he engaged with in each country: "Back in Cloloa Pushta [*sic*], I played the Super Mario games. When I left Afghanistan the first place I went was to Pakistan. In Pakistan I watched Dragonball Z. Also in Canada, I started watching Naruto Uzumaki."

As described earlier, there were gender differences in how the students demonstrated continuity and evolution in their stories of migration. Whereas boys (like Abdullah in Figure 5) tended to use video games, TV, and films to drive the narrative, girls tended to use flora, fauna, and landscape to link their experiences in two (or more) countries. Regardless of the technique chosen, all students were able to demonstrate the ability to sequence events in their digital narratives; a lack of English proficiency might have precluded them from doing so in a traditional text-based narrative. These digital stories also provided authentic teachable moments for introducing sequencing vocabulary such as *next, then,* and *finally.*

Vocabulary Building, Use of Figurative Speech, and Literary Devices

The Language Curriculum document (Ontario Ministry of Education, 2006) developed for native speakers of English is the curriculum to which advanced ELLs in Ontario transition as their proficiency becomes increasingly native-like. Its expectations for student writing include an increasing ability to use vivid and/or figurative language and innovative expressions to enhance interest. Suggested techniques for accomplishing this end include comparative and unusual adjectives and adverbs, similes, personification, metaphor, and unexpected word order. The invitation to experiment with language in this way typically comes at the cost of grammar conventions, because incorporating these stylistic techniques in complex sentences requires a sophisticated knowledge of the mechanics of the language. In a multimodal text, however, the images support the writer by freeing him or her from the need to establish the context, thereby allowing for experimentation with figurative speech in isolation from complex grammatical constraints.

Of the 18 ELLs in the study, only 2 had advanced levels English proficiency—one (Daniel) possibly due to having been in Canada longer than the others, and the other (Abdullah) due perhaps to having strong interpersonal skills (as observed by one of the researchers). In his digital narrative, Abdullah described a burning sun and a rushing ocean; Daniel described circling fish and masked monsters (see Figure 6). For each of these students, the selected images both elicited and scaffolded the use of compelling and descriptive adjectives. In addition, Daniel used a metaphor to relate his personal identity exploration to his love of anime: "I am from worlds of fantasy and reality slipping from one into the other. Reality or fantasy its [sic] all the same to me" (see Figure 7).

Developing Digital Literacy Skills

Although students need to develop the skills and knowledge to use a variety of digital media software applications and hardware devices, digital literacy goes beyond simple technology skills. It also includes the ability to critically understand digital media content and applications and the knowledge and capacity to create such content with digital technology. It is imperative that students be able to express themselves through multiple modes that go beyond print text. Thus, we examined the work of participants through the following foci, which integrate standards established by both NCTE (2008) and ISTE (2012):

- proficiency with the tools of technology
- collaboration and communication when engaged in problem solving and decision making
- synthesis of multiple streams of information presented simultaneously in different modalities
- critique, analysis, and evaluation of multimedia texts
- digital citizenship

In this small-scale study, students learned simple computer commands and how to use Windows Movie Maker or Microsoft Photo Story software. However, the task also required them to navigate websites and scan the images found there, browse various sources and select a focus, retrieve relevant and appropriate

Figure 6. Use of Adjectives by Abdullah and Daniel to Enrich Descriptive Text

images or music to support their story or poem, and finally communicate their understanding through a variety of modes of expression. While searching for the "right" images, students had to evaluate each image in terms of its usefulness, appropriateness, and relevance in the context of their story or poem. In the creation of the digital texts, students had to synthesize multiple streams of information presented via different modalities, deciding how the images, text, and sound would work together to create meaning and communicate their intentions to an audience. Finally, students learned about copyright while searching for images, which is part of digital citizenship. In sum, despite the fact that most of the digital texts were quite simple, and the students had limited prior experience using computer technology, the nature of this highly motivating production process required the development and use of a number of digital literacy skills.

Figure 7. Figurative Speech Used by Daniel to Explore Identity

CONCLUSION

Linguistic diversity has become the reality in most schools serving urban areas. Classroom teachers who are mandated to teach to the "whole child" can no longer rely exclusively on language to learn about the students in their classrooms. Multimodal teacher-assigned identity texts in the form of personal narratives and poetry allow ELLs to construct and convey their dynamic, hybrid identities without the constraints of composing exclusively in a language that is not their mother tongue. Norton Peirce (1995) argues that "it is through language that a person negotiates a sense of self within and across different sites" and "gains access to— or is denied access to—powerful social networks" (p. 13), but we would add that multimedia tools are another viable means to accomplish this end and should therefore be integrated into classes with ELLs.

As explained by Albers and Sanders (2010),

> We know that when people are actively engaged with inquiry, have a desire to learn new things, and try out different digital, visual, musical, spatial, dramatic (and so on) tools and techniques, they have the potential to say and do things we have never before imagined. (p. 3)

Students were invited to share their digital stories and poems with teachers, peers, and parents. Through informal discussions with the students and their teachers afterwards, creating and sharing digital texts in this project appeared to result in the empowerment of newly constructed student identities, including entitlement to claims of being legitimate English speakers, writers/poets/artists, digital citizens, and new Canadians. Furthermore, these digital texts seemed to facilitate the acquisition of English language skills required by curriculum expectations. As users, producers, and critics of their own media, the ELLs in this study were highly motivated to learn how to organize and convey their ideas effectively and clearly. Teachers of English across all grade levels should be encouraged to incorporate digital multimedia projects into their classrooms. The case study presented in this chapter suggests many potential benefits for English language learners in moving beyond traditional oral and text-based narratives and overly simplistic conceptualizations of literacy.

CHAPTER 5

English Learning Through Arts, Music, and Digital Media: A Photostory Project

Aiden Yeh

This chapter shares effective practices on blending learning by providing an overview of a collaborative photostory project designed for intermediate English as a foreign language (EFL) learners, which integrates visual arts, English language songs, and digital media. Two student-produced photostories are also discussed to illustrate the learning process or the different project stages in which students applied the skills that they had learned and to show examples of language and visual interpretations. This project shows that photostories can be effectively used in capturing the essence of an artist's work, creatively incorporating music, lyrics, and visual illustrations that put the pieces of art together in one storyline that captivates the audience's heart and imagination.

The use of visual arts and music in language learning is nothing new. A number of research studies have suggested the positive learning outcomes of using music in the English language classroom. Based on a study conducted among students learning English as a second language, listening to a song was ranked by students as the top most enjoyable activity (Lems, 2005). Another study found that music has an affective effect on students' language production, because "the more communicative and student centered activities such as music [and] conversation . . . were more memorable, effective and favorable than more conventional, teacher initiated activities such as research and report" (Reimann, 2002, p. 5). Visual arts are useful in language learning because they serve as effective tools or aids for communicative or writing tasks (Gairns & Redman, 1986). Art is a visual language; perception, imagination, and the ability to analyze and interpret are being merged in the process of interacting with the artwork. Students use some of these same skills when learning how to read and write in a nonnative language. The photostory project discussed in this chapter is relevant to language teachers because it shows how music and visual arts can be creatively integrated into one task-based activity; this class project also demonstrates the use of new technologies in the traditional face-to-face language learning environment to help students complete the task.

This chapter shares effective practices by providing an overview of a collaborative photostory project designed for intermediate-level EFL students that integrates visual arts, English language songs, and digital media using PowerPoint and Windows Movie Maker. The students' learning context and needs and the integration of project-based learning assessment are discussed. Two student-produced videos are used as case studies in analyzing interpretations of music, lyrics, and images that are visually and emotionally captivating. The end product reveals that students had a good grasp of the learning task process of putting visual images, sound, and lyrics together to tell a story, to create a mood or feeling that viewers come to associate with their personal experiences. This project focused primarily on enhancing the students' English language skills (reading, writing, listening, and speaking) and application of computer skills.

CONTEXT AND PARTICIPANTS

Internet English is a compulsory 2-credit yearlong course offered to English-major freshmen at a private college in southern Taiwan. Its objective is to further develop students' listening, speaking, reading, and writing skills through a variety of activities using Internet resources while also enhancing their technical skills. This course covers various thematically organized topics such as current events, social issues, literature, and poetry.

The participants involved in the photostory project were English-major freshman students enrolled in this course, which I taught. The students were divided into two class sections: Undergraduate English 1A (UE1A) and Undergraduate English 1B (UE1B).[1] Each class has 50 students, for a total of 100. Three were international students (2 from Indonesia and 1 from South Korea), and the rest were students from Taiwan whose native language was Mandarin Chinese. Students' previous knowledge or experience related to the use of technology was not a factor in the selection process.

CLASSROOM SETUP: SUPPORTING
A BLENDED LEARNING ENVIRONMENT

The classroom setup made it easier to create a blended learning environment where the use of online technology was integrated into all learning activities. Face-to-face class meetings were held regularly in a computer laboratory with access to the Internet, but a Yahoo! Group (YG) was still created for each class to maintain online communication via the email-based messaging system. The students were invited to join the class YG to keep abreast of what was happening in class. The syllabus and learning materials were archived in the files area of the

---

[1] The names of the classes in Mandarin Chinese are 日四技英文—A (UE1A) and 日四技英文—B (UE1B).

YG, and links to various websites used in class were bookmarked in the Links area. The constant updates and reminders via the class YG enhanced student–student and student–teacher rapport. The messages posted on the YG suggested such rapport through the sharing of personal information, ideas, and opinions. In addition, the informal personal discussions on the YG were also recognized as indicators of positive rapport.

Class wikis[2] were also created and used to publish learning materials and exhibit student-produced projects. The class wikis were updated weekly, and students were automatically notified about the updates by email. The use of blogs was also an important element of the course. Students were taught how to create and maintain their individual blogs at the start of the semester (see Appendix A). They were introduced to Blogger (www.blogger.com), but they were also encouraged to use their own existing blogs if they had any. The students' individual blogs served as learning portfolios where they could archive work that exhibited their skills; their blogs showcased everything that they had accomplished in the course, including their tasks on the photostory project. To keep track of all the students' blogs, the URLs (i.e., web addresses) of their blogs were added to the Links area of the class YG. In addition, we subscribed to blog feeds (i.e., data generated from blog updates) using Protopage (www.protopage .com/internet_english_ue1a), which showed snippets of all the students' blogs on a single page. This allowed us to check the students' assigned blog entries without having to go through all the links.

In preparation for the photostory project, students were also introduced to audio and video podcasting weeks before their expected in-class presentations (see Appendix A). Students learned how to do their own voice recording and publish it on a podcast server and on their blogs. The online video servers Blip (http://blip.tv) and Internet Archive (http://archive.org/) were used to store these podcasts, and students could share them with each other by embedding links on their own blogs. The entire process of producing podcasts enhanced students' English language skills (reading, writing, listening, and speaking). Students also received training on the creative elements of PowerPoint to produce photostories. Visual aids used during student presentations and PowerPoint lecture materials were uploaded online using SlideBoom (www.slideboom.com), which was also embedded on the class wiki.

THE PHOTOSTORY PROJECT

The photostory project was created using PowerPoint and Windows Movie Maker. Because this task was given as a midterm project, it was vital to have 4 weeks of preparation to make sure that students had ample time to finish their work (see Timeline in Appendix A). Examples of previous student-produced photostories

---

[2] See http://ue1a.pbworks.com and http://ue1b.pbworks.com.

were shown to students in order to model how photostories are created as well as how background music and visuals can be integrated to construct a story that reflects an artist's life or artwork. A hands-on workshop was given in a computer lab to teach students how to use PowerPoint and Windows Movie Maker (see Microsoft, 2012; Template Ready, n.d.). The instructional material was also made available online via the class YG and wiki. Students were given enough time to complete the photostory task outside the classroom.

Photostory Project Concept

For the photostory project, students were required to create one 5-minute audio-visual resource about an artist of their choice. Their work had to include any type of music that reflected the mood of the artist's work. This project required group work for successful completion of the task; the class was divided into 12 groups, each of which had approximately five members. Students had 3 weeks to complete the project in their own time. Group work was deemed most appropriate because it adheres to a socioconstructivist teaching approach that engages students' negotiation of meaning and of technology (Vygotsky, 1978).

A photostory is defined as the arrangement of songs (in this case, English language songs) and photographs or digital images of illustrations, drawings, sketches, or any visual artwork in a creative manner to tell a compelling story. A photostory resembles a music video; a new twist is added to the song's lyrics by using visual imagery to represent their message. If the message of the song presented in the lyrics is supported or highlighted by a matching visual, it creates a new dimension of experience for the audience. This project required that students develop the ability to tell a story using images. The students had dealt with visual arts in the past, but instead of creating or drawing on their own artwork for the present project, they made use of work produced by other artists. Out of the many art pieces available to them, they chose a few illustrations that would help them tell a story. In other words, students learned how to read illustrations critically and understand the themes portrayed in the images. This included, for example, paying attention to artists' use of colors to convey emotions in their work.

As students learned to read, interpret, and communicate visually, they also needed to apply their skills in critical literacy to examine a text for its tacit meanings (Rosenblatt, 1995). To understand the lyrics of songs in English, students had to understand their meaning by going through the words or phrases, interpreting the information contained in them, and making sure that this information resonated with the message conveyed by the images they chose. In addition, students focused their attention on the fundamental storytelling elements involved. According to Lidwell, Holden, and Butler (2003), these elements are setting, characters, plot, invisibility, mood, and movement (see Table 1).

The successful execution of the project started with good planning and well-crafted scripts or storyboards. According to Rosales (2006), the storyboard gives

Table 1. Elements of Storytelling

Setting	The setting orients the audience, providing a sense of time and place for the story.
Characters	Character identification is how the audience becomes involved in the story and how the story becomes relevant.
Plot	The plot ties the events in the story together and is the channel through which the story can flow.
Invisibility	The awareness of the storyteller fades as the audience focuses on a good story. The existence of the medium is forgotten.
Mood	Music, lighting, and style of prose create the emotional tone of the story.
Movement	In a good story, the sequence and flow of events is clear and interesting. The storyline does not stall.

Source: Adapted from Lidwell et al. (2003, p. 186).

students a sense of the vision of the project and the end result they are trying to achieve. In creating scripts and storyboards, students needed to pay careful attention to two essential elements: their choice of artist, including his or her style or philosophy in creating art, and their choice of music, including melody and lyrics (see Table 2). Both the melody and lyrics had to be analyzed when choosing background music. The lyrics needed to match the visual art so students could

Table 2. The Task

The Artist
1. If you were to introduce an artist, who would you choose and why?
2. Choose an artist (someone who paints) and provide information about him or her.
3. Provide reasons why you chose this artist.
4. Describe this artist's art. What is his or her style or philosophy in creating art?
5. Show one or two examples of your artist's art.

The Art
6. Create a short photostory (2–3 minutes) using PowerPoint or Movie Maker.
7. Include pictures of the artist's work.
8. Choose background music that expresses any or all of the following:
• the theme of the artist's work
• the artist's personality
• any aspect of the artist's work, life, or both
9. Listen to and understand the lyrics. What is the music telling you, and how does it match the illustrations that you will be showing?
10. Use the Van Gogh photostory as an example.

create a coherent 2- to 3-minute photostory using PowerPoint or Movie Maker. The background music needed to express any or all of the following aspects:

- the theme of the artist's work

- the artist's personality

- any aspect of the artist's work, life, or both

Classroom Pretask Activity

The process began with students participating in a pretask mini-workshop that covered song interpretation, sample photostories, the use of multimedia tools, and the task guidelines. For the song interpretation activity, I used Cindi Lauper's "True Colors" (Steinberg & Kelly, 1986). The students were asked to listen to the song and try to understand the message of the lyrics. They then completed a short paper-based cloze exercise (see Appendix B). The music was played twice, after which students checked their answers, occasionally pausing to look up word spellings and definitions. This activity took 15 minutes to complete. Once students had created a complete copy of the lyrics, the song was played one last time. Students were then guided to reflect on the meaning of the lyrics. They had 15 minutes to respond to the following writing prompt:

> Based on your interpretation of the song, what does "true colors" mean? In your opinion, what is the story/message behind the lyrics (words) of the song? Can you relate your personal experiences to the song's message? Write a brief paragraph, and post it on your blog.

The following excerpt is an example of a blog entry that shows the student's articulate expression of her personal interpretation of the song.

> Tuesday, October 7, 2008, True Colours
>
> To me, "True Colours" means a person's characteristics or the dream one wishes to come true. The message behind the lyrics of this song is to encourage people to be themsleves [*sic*] and live their dreams instead of holding yourself down to meet other people's expectations. In my own experience, there were times when I had to do things the way other people wanted from me even though I tried to speak my mind. Sometimes it is difficult to show one's "true colours" if you take into consideration the possibility of being spoken of as unrealistic or inconsiderate of others.

For the remaining 30 minutes of the class, students discussed the photostory project. A photostory about Vincent Van Gogh, which reflected the artist's severe depression by combining images of his paintings with Don Mclean's (1971) song "Vincent" (also known as "Starry, Starry Night"), was used as an example. After watching the Van Gogh photostory in class, students discussed the elements that make a good photostory and how background music and visuals can be integrated to create a story that reflects the artist's life and artwork.

Adopting Lidwell and colleagues' (2003) concept of storytelling, students explored the elements that make a good story. The images selected from Van Gogh's paintings told a compelling story about the crucial point in the artist's life when he "lost his sanity" and how his perceptions of his own surroundings were depicted in his paintings. The lyrics perfectly synchronized with the famous artworks of Van Gogh; for example, the lines "Starry, starry night. Paint your palette blue and gray" describe Van Gogh's painting "Starry Night." The swirling lines of the sky were painted using the colors blue and gray. The whorls and twisted lines that illustrate the evening skies are possible representations of his mental state. Van Gogh's self-portrait was presented with the line "With eyes that know the darkness in my soul"; the painting shows Van Gogh's dark eyes staring and gives the viewers the impression that he is looking at them directly. The photostory image also focuses on Van Gogh's eyes in the painting, provoking the viewer to look at his eyes and see who he really is. Each line or verse of the song uses concise language to deliver a crucial piece of a story around a unified theme. The use of images helps the viewer visualize this story; in this example, the images are surreal, realistic, or impressionistic interpretations of life. The meaning and depth of Van Gogh's artwork deepens as one repeatedly listens to and watches the photostory; the art pieces work together with the lyrics to tell the story of a life filled with sadness and pain.

Task Planning

The second step in the process divided students into small groups to brainstorm, plan, and gather sufficient information to help them select their topic and task strategy. Using online search engines, they researched local and international artists. Students' choice of artist was submitted and placed on a topic list that was sent to the entire class via the YG. All group representatives posted to the YG a list of group members as well as their choice of artist and song. This list made it easy to double-check which groups had the same topic. If this situation occurred, the decision of which group was allowed to pursue a topic was based on a first-come-first-served basis, and this could be verified by checking the time that each message was posted in the YG archive.

The students had to make use of the remaining 2–3 weeks to work on their presentation materials outside the classroom. During this time, students wrote and edited their scripts, selected visual graphics and background music, and combined all materials into their final photostory presentation. In-class presentations of the projects were held in the computer lab during two 2-hour class meetings. Each group was given approximately 10–15 minutes per meeting to present. Appendix C shows a complete list of artists and songs chosen by the students.

Criteria for Assessment

Task assessment addressed three modes of communication: interpersonal, interpretive, and presentational. These modes place emphasis on the context and purpose of communication, whereby students are expected to use either oral or written language for sharing information and opinions, interpreting concepts, and developing ideas (National Standards in Foreign Language Education Project, 1999). The interpersonal mode requires active negotiation of meaning among individuals (e.g., face-to-face communication), the interpretative mode is characterized by the interpretation of meanings that occur in written or spoken form (e.g., reading a story, listening to music, watching a film or video), and the presentational mode focuses on the creation of spoken or written messages (e.g., written or oral reports that facilitate and affirm student interpretations).

One of the key points in assessment was whether the students would be able to clearly convey the message of the visual presentation to the audience. Students had to pay attention to the language in their oral presentation as well as the interpretation of their photostory language (i.e., music, lyrics, and images). They were required to use descriptive language to describe the artist's life and work and to present strong position statements in defending their choice of artist and song. For the photostory language interpretation, students had to have a deep understanding of the message of the song, beyond the literal definition of the lyrics, and apply that understanding by matching them with appropriate visuals from their chosen artist's collection of works.

Copies of the self-made rubric (see Figure 1) were distributed to the students as soon as the task assignment was given. The rubric was also posted on the class wiki. With the task criteria clearly stated in the rubric, students were aware of what they needed to do in order to meet the task requirements. The rubric also provided objective information with which to evaluate students' skills, and it served as a checklist when producing their projects.

In measuring the effectiveness of the photostory project, I looked at how successful the students were in completing the task. Using the criteria stated in the rubric, it was evident from observations that students met or exceeded all task requirements. Most groups earned a high score, indicating that their presentations were exemplary.

Clearly identifying the task criteria during the pretask activity meant that the students had a list of benchmarks to guide them through the process. They knew that the careful selection of a suitable song was pertinent, as was the selection of images. A poor choice of image that did not resonate with the overall meaning of the song could leave the audience feeling confused. As one of the students pointed out during his presentation,

> One of the task requirements should show the relevance and connection between
> the words expressed in the song and the visuals being shown. In our group's case,
> we put great care in matching Jimmy's paintings with the lyrics. Both the lyrics and

Group: _____
Choice of Painter/Artist: _____
Choice of Music: _____
Grade Key: E= Excellent, G= Good, A= Average, P=Poor

Criteria	Grade	Comments
Language and the Painter/Artist Discussed reasons for choosing the artist Provided sufficient background information about the artist's life (key events in life) Described artist's art, style, creative philosophy Showed ample examples of artist's work		
Language and Music Choice of song that expressed one or all of the following: • Theme of the artist's work • Artist's personality • Any aspect of the artist's work and/or life Creative interpretation of the lyrics (song's message) and visual imagery (using the artist's paintings or art work) Was the choice of song appropriate?		
Oral Presentation Organization Preparation Language Use Powerpoint Presentation Material Creative use of bullets to highlight points Creative design Delivery Skills Spontaneous (or Monotonous Reading?) Entertaining and informative		
Collaborative Work		
Grade =		

Other comments

Figure 1. Rubric for the Photostory Project

the pictures that we presented showed love, peace, and warmth because that's what Jimmy's work is about: loving relationships. And I believe that our group was able to effectively show that.

ANALYSIS OF THE PHOTOSTORY METHOD

Using the three communication modes in assessing the students' performance and educational gains in terms of language learning, it was evident that this project provided many opportunities for students to enhance their use of English.

Interpersonal

In the face-to-face classroom presentations, students were engaged in two-way interactive communication between groups of students (i.e., between presenters and the rest of the class). The class listened to the presenters as they made their points across various issues about the song or the theme of the photostory.

Furthermore, the unscripted discussion sessions following presentations allowed students to converse in a spontaneous way.

Presentational

Groups of students created PowerPoint presentations to introduce the artist and the songwriter or singer that they had chosen. During the presentation, students elaborated on their chosen works of art and discussed reasons for their choice of artist, song, and images. They also described the artwork and the artist's philosophy of art. Figure 2 is a snapshot of four PowerPoint slides that clearly illustrates the kinds of critical information the students presented. The first two slides show a picture of the artist and some of his biographical information, and the other two slides depict reasons why students chose that artist.

The student-produced photostories showcased what they had learned linguistically and artistically. To be able to put together the photostory, the students needed to read a large amount of information in English about the artists and their work. They also had to write their reports and give an oral presentation in English. The overall impact of the photostory on the audience necessarily drew on the students' understanding of the lyrics and their ability to present interdisciplinary concepts, knowledge, and skills. Thus, the positive audience reactions to the photostories that I observed provided evidence of presenters' comprehension of their topics in English in addition to their presentational abilities.

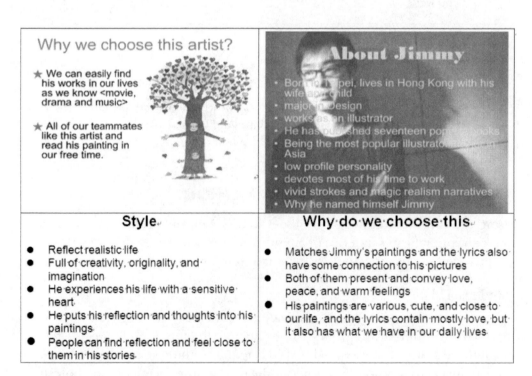

Figure 2. Snapshots of Students' PowerPoint Slides About an Artist

Interpretive

The coherence of each student-produced photostory depended on how well students understood and interpreted the message of the song. Achieving consistency between the song and images in the photostory required students to actively explore the meaning of the music by listening to the song, reading the lyrics, categorizing the words and images, and ultimately making connections between the newly gathered information and existing background knowledge. In this highly interpretive process, students also acquired new vocabulary and new phrases to express themselves through photostories.

TWO CASE STUDIES OF PHOTOSTORIES

This section presents two student-produced photostories (one from each class), which were chosen to provide clear examples of language and visual interpretations. Both projects featured the same local artist, but the choices of music and photostory theme were different (see Table 3). Both photostories captured the essence of the artist's work, creatively incorporating music and visual illustrations in a coherent storyline that captivated the audience.

Both groups chose to focus on a renowned Taiwanese author-illustrator named Jimmy Liao, who is particularly famous among the current young adult generation. Liao's illustration styles, as the students pointed out in their oral presentations, are very much grounded in reality, so it is often not difficult for the audience to relate to his work. Student presenters also showed Liao's official website and pointed out that the artist makes use of images as a new form of

Table 3. Comparison of Two Photostories Based on Jimmy Liao's Illustrations

Group	UE1A	UE1B
Artist	Jimmy Liao	Jimmy Liao
Song	"At the End of the Day," by Emi Fujita (see lyrics in Appendix D)	"Home," by Michael Bublé (see lyrics in Appendix E)
Photostory theme	Unexpressed love and the need for companionship; choices people make affect destiny	Being far away from someone you love; missing home
Main characters	A boy and a girl	A boy and a girl
Plot	A girl in the midst of the hustle and bustle of city life is caught desperately struggling to overcome loneliness as she yearns for a boy who can offer her companionship.	A boy and a girl who are a thousand miles apart are fighting to overcome the distance for their love to survive.

literary language with a charming poetic appeal. The *Taipei Times* published a positive critique of Liao's illustrated books, commenting that they have

> become a big hit by luring office workers, housewives and other grown-ups back to the days when drawings outnumbered the words in the books they enjoyed. His illustrated books contain simple stories about people coping in the modern urban world. ("Making Picture Books for Adults," paras. 2–3)

China Youth Daily also stated, "Jimmy's drawing touches the hearts of urban youth. It relieves the fears and anxieties of urbanites, who are living amid struggle and pressure" ("Making Picture Books for Adults," para. 3). These were the same reasons the students chose Jimmy Liao's art work; they felt that Liao's artistic style could be described as cute, whimsical, and cartoon-like and credited his success in conveying people's feelings and moods to his simplistic style. Most of the illustrations that the students used were from Liao's collection of illustrated books (i.e., *A Chance of Sunshine* [2000], *The Sound of Colors* [2006; with Thompson], *The Fish With a Smile* [2009], and *Never Ending Story* [2006]) because these images matched the lyrics and message of the songs that they had chosen.

The group from UE1A chose a slow, romantic song, "At the End of the Day," sung by Emi Fujita, which focuses on love and companionship (see Appendix D), whereas the group from UE1B chose a ballad by Michael Bublé called "Home," which also draws on the theme of love, but deals more with how it feels to be away from a loved one (see Appendix E).

The photostory of the UE1A group consists of 26 slides; the first 25 show illustrations of the artist along with corresponding lines of text taken from the song's lyrics; the last slide shows a list of group members and their contributions to the project. It took each group 6–8 hours spread across 3 weeks to complete the photostory. The storyboard presented by the group from UE1A shows the first few lines of the song "At the End of the Day." The first slide contains the title "Jimmy," which immediately suggests to the audience that the photostory contains the illustrations of Jimmy Liao and his views on love. The text in Slide 2, "Well my days went by at a dizzying pace," is matched with an image of a girl standing in a train or subway station. The trains coming and going in this slide suggest a busy and fast-paced way of life. This is how the day went by for this girl, as is further suggested in the lyrics, "I was always running to and fro." In the next image, the same girl is seen at a crossroads where stairways from different directions offer her choices, but the location itself looks surreal, suggesting unfamiliarity and thus corresponding to the lyrics "and then before I even knew where I was." This image also demonstrates that the students looked beyond the literal translation of the song; the crossroads could signify one's unknown destiny and that life can take a whole different direction based on the choices that one makes. The next scene shows the girl setting birds free, which could be interpreted as wanting to have the freedom to fly or follow her dreams, hence the line "off to dreamland I would go." A later slide features a dreary, grey, and empty park with the girl on top of a leafless tree, reflecting a deep interpretation of the text "but now I realize that a day of my life is the price I must pay for tomorrow." The student authors were suggesting that if the girl in the lyrics continues on her present course, she may find herself alone in a dreary world such as this.

The idea of having a male companion is presented in an illustration, which shows a boy sharing his coat with a girl to protect her from the rain. This image fit well with the line "You have taught me to treasure every day, with its joy and its sorrow"; "you" refers to the boy in the drawing who protects her by telling her to value each day. The lyrics "you know that I'm the one who's always swept away, always torn apart" suggest that the girl is somewhat weak and emotionally torn. The text "how I wish that there was something I could do for you," and the corresponding image of a boy with his arm extended, both suggest that the boy would respond to her call for help. As the song segues to the third verse, "simply from my heart, darling at the close of day, silently for love we'll pray," the illustration then features both the boy and the girl sitting silently by a riverbank. In the background are two big hearts formed by deformed tree trunks, suggesting that love is in the air—though not verbally expressed, it is strongly felt by the couple as they sit together.

The group from UE1B used a total of 47 slides in their photostory, 42 of which contain illustrations from Liao, the artist. This group also spent 6–8 hours spread across 3 weeks creating their photostory. The first 6 slides contain the introduction of their presentation, which included the title page showing a picture of the illustrator, Jimmy Liao; pictures of the group members who contributed to the creation of the photostory; and a picture of the singer, Michael Bublé, and the title of the song, "Home." This song's lyrics tell a story about a man missing the person he loves dearly because she is so far away.

The first line of the lyrics, "Another summer day," is matched with an illustration of the sun. For the second line, "has come and gone away," the corresponding image depicts a drawing of a girl who has carved the shape of her body in a tall hedge, leaving her imprint to prove that she was once there. The line "In Paris and Rome, I wanna go home" suggests the idea of traveling and is matched with a picture of a bus. The illustration used with the line "maybe surrounded by a million people" is a literal interpretation that shows a crowd of people. Despite being surrounded by people, the character in the song still feels alone, a feeling conveyed in the photostory through a picture of a man alone in an empty field. The song's first verse ends with the line "I just wanna go home," and the illustration shows a girl standing against a post, deep in thought. The photostory shows how the character in the song misses her loved one by depicting a woman looking at a mounted picture of the man she loves. The next slides used by the group tell the audience how the character tries to send letters, sometimes sending messages in a bottle—a meaning that is clearly conveyed in both the lyrics and the illustrations. However, the truth still remains that sending letters is not enough, since words can sometimes be "cold and flat." Overall, the song intimates that physical presence is important in maintaining a relationship, which is well expressed by the students' photostory.

CONCLUSION

People relate their own personal experiences (e.g., in love and relationships) to the lyrics of songs, and listening to songs can thus be very effective for meaningful language learning. In this case study, music interpretation activities that involved the reading of lyrics and images prompted in-class discussions, and using blogs as tools for students to post their opinions about a topic shared in class gave students opportunities to enhance their writing skills. The photostory project provided a creative avenue for students to learn to express their understanding and appreciation of art, music, and lyrics. Assessments based on task performance facilitated authentic interactions using the target language. Students were evaluated based on the quality of their oral presentations, their report papers, and the collaborative execution of their projects. Students also saw what other groups had created and how they performed, thus providing them with further opportunities to reflect on the outcomes of their own projects. The final product helped students demonstrate their understanding of a formidable quantity of information and resources, engage in the negotiation of meaning, and utilize previous knowledge to define photostory themes and concepts.

The process of creating a photostory using English songs and images allowed students to apply their linguistic, artistic, and critical thinking skills to a creative art project. Furthermore, the project motivated students to think about the real world around them as they tried to integrate different language skills into their interpretations of music and art in order to create a meaningful photostory. Finally, students had the opportunity to engage in Internet research and work with a range of digital media tools, from simple PowerPoint presentations to more advanced applications such as Windows Movie Maker. Students were able to produce and present photostory videos that exhibited unique interpretations of art pieces, music, lyrics, and images and were both visually and emotionally captivating. As a result, the photostory project effectively facilitated students' interaction with and production of English.

APPENDIX A:
COURSE SYLLABUS FOR THE FIRST SEMESTER

上課日期 Date	課程內容 Course Content	授課方式 Instructional Approaches	作業、報告、考試或其他 Assignments, Tests and Others	備註 Remarks	
9/8~ 9/13 Week 1	Course Introduction Introducing Yahoo!Groups	Lecture, Discussion, hands-on workshop	Write a brief self-introduction (individual)	9/8 No class (Orientation)	
9/15~ 9/20 Week 2	E-Portfolio Blogging Learning how to write blog entries, comments, and feedback	Lecture, Discussion, hands-on workshop	Create e-portfolio Writing blog entries (individual) Assignment: Local News: sinlaku	Blogs and E-portfolio must be maintained and updated weekly	
9/22~ 9/27 Week 3	Social Networking	Lecture, Discussion, hands-on workshop	Create individual account in Facebook and Twitter News: Tainted milk		
9/29~ 10/4 Week 4	Creating a Photostory photostory	Lecture, Discussion, hands-on	Assign groupings true_colors		Project Preparation: Introduction Lyrics and Music: Understanding the message behind the words (lyrics) Creating a photostory using music and visuals
10/6~ 10/11 Week 5	Podcasting (Audio/Video) 10 things about learning English that make you happy. podcasting	Lecture, Discussion, hands-on workshop	Create audio podcast, embed it on blog	10/10 Double Tenth Day (Fri. – day off)	
10/13~ 10/18 Week 6	Audio Discussion Forum News Online (CNN, BBC, CBS, etc)	Lecture, Discussion, hands-on workshop	Join voice discussion on Chinswing	doh	
10/20~ 10/25 Week 7	Audio Discussion Forum News Online (CNN, BBC, CBS, etc)	Lecture, Discussion, hands-on workshop	Creating-News-Podcast	Radio-TV-Podcast	
10/27~ 11/1 Week 8	Photostory Project Presentation Photostory_Students_Projects		Groups 1-5	Rubric	Project Presentations
11/3~ 11/8 Week 9	**Midterm Exam** **Photostory Project Presentation**		Groups 6-10		
11/10~ 11/15	Groups 11-13 presentations Message_to_Obama	Lecture, Discussion, hands-on workshop	Weekly reflections, comments, and feedback on the blog and audio forum	Video conferences with international participants (to be confirmed)	
11/17~ 11/22	whats-in-a-name What-to-wear	Presentation & discussion			
11/24~ 11/29	Weekly podcast shows T1: Forever Single Forever_Single_Podcast T2: Taking care of mother	Presentation & discussion	Group-presenters-self-evaluations		

APPENDIX B:
"TRUE COLORS" LANGUAGE ACTIVITY

(Steinberg & Kelly, 1986)

You with the [1] _____, don't be discouraged
Oh I realize it's hard to take [2] _____
In a world full of people you can lose sight of it all
And the [3] _____ inside you can make you feel so small

But I see your true colors [4] _____ through
I see your true colors and that's why I love you
So don't be [5] _____ to let them show
Your true colors, true colors are beautiful, like a [6] _____

Show me a smile then, don't be [7] _____,
Can't remember when I last saw you laughing
If this world makes you [8] _____
And you've taken all you can bear
You call me up because you know I'll be there

But I see your true colors [9] _____ through
I see your true colors and that's why I love you
So don't be [10] _____ to let them show
Your true colors, true colors are beautiful, like a [11] _____

(when I last saw you laughing)
If this world makes you crazy
And you've taken all you can [12] _____
You call me up because you know I'll be there

And I see your [13] _____ shining through
I see your true colors and that's why I love you
So don't be afraid to let them [14] _____
Your true colors, true colors, true colors
Shining through
I see your true colors and that's why I love you
So don't be afraid to let them show
Your true colors, true colors are beautiful,
Like a [15] _____

APPENDIX C:
LIST OF STUDENTS' PROJECTS

Artist	Song
1. Michelangelo	"I'm Yours," by Jason Mraz
2. Egon Schiele	"I Wish I Knew How It Would Feel to Be Free," by Lighthouse Family
3. Frida Kahlo	"The Floating Bed," by Elliot Goldenthal
4. Jimmy Liao (Local Artist)	"At the End of the Day," by Emi Fujita
5. Jean Fransois Millet	"Take Me Home," by John Denver
6. Edward Munch	"What I've Done," by Linkin Park
7. Leonardo da Vinci	"Top of the World," by The Carpenters
8. Edgar Degas	"Tiny Dancer," by Elton John
9. Henri Matisse	"Dream On," by Aerosmith
10. Renoir	"In a Big World," by Emilia
11. Toulouse Lautrec	"Dancing Queen," by Abba
12. Constable	"Moon River," by Johnny Mercer

APPENDIX D:
"AT THE END OF THE DAY" LYRICS

(Fujita, 2012)

Well, my days went by at a dizzying pace
I was always running to and fro
And then before I even knew where I was
Off to dreamland I would go

But now I realize that a day of my life
Is the price I must pay for tomorrow
You have taught me to treasure every day
With its joy and its sorrow

You know that I'm
the one who's always being swept away
Always torn apart

How I wish that there was something
I could do for you
Simply from my heart
Darling, at the close of day
Silently for love we'll pray

Now night has finally come to the busy city sky
Where quietly the moon is shining down
On the paths of people hurrying home
She sheds her light all around

And in this heart of mine your love is shining down
It's lighting up my future and my past
That is the reason I'm living now
Treating each day as my last

And if you want to know the reason I'm crying, dear
It's 'cause I love you so
How I wish that there was something
I could do for you
Just to let it show
Darling, at the close of day, silently for love we'll pray

Now if you want to know the reason I'm crying, dear
It's 'cause I love you so
How I wish that there was something
I could do for you
Just to let it show
Tomorrow's just a dream away,
Close the curtain on today

APPENDIX E:
"HOME" LYRICS

(Bublé, Chang, & Foster-Gillies, 2005)

Another summer day
has come and gone away
In Paris or Rome . . .
but I wanna go home
. . . uhm Home
may be surrounded by
a million people
I still feel all alone
just wanna go home
I miss you, you know

And I've been keeping all the letters
that I wrote to you,
Each one a line or two
I'm fine baby, how are you?
I would send them but I know that it's just not enough
My words were cold and flat
And you deserve more than that

Another aeroplane, another sunny place,
I'm lucky I know
but I wanna go home
I got to go home

Let me go home

I'm just too far from where you are
I wanna come home

And I feel just like I'm living
someone else's life
It's like I just stepped outside
when everything was going right
And I know just why you could not come along with me
This was not your dream
but you always believed in me . . .

Another winter day
Has come and gone away
in either Paris or Rome
and I wanna go home
Let me go home

And I'm surrounded by
A million people
I still feel alone
Let me go home
I miss you, you know

Let me go home
I've had my run
Baby I'm done
I gotta go home

Let me go home
It'll all be alright
I'll be home tonight
I'm coming back home

CHAPTER 6

A Project-Based Approach to Vocabulary Acquisition: Filmmaking With ESL Students

Jia Li and Brenda McComb

Research has shown that both domestic and international undergraduate English as a second language (ESL) students in Canadian universities face formidable challenges in understanding course lectures, participating in classroom activities, reading assigned materials, and writing essays. Many of these problems can be traced to a lack of vocabulary in academic contexts. However, few studies are available that investigate innovative interventions designed to facilitate ESL students' learning of English vocabulary to bridge their English proficiency gaps.

This chapter examines the impact on English learning, and in particular, on vocabulary acquisition, of engaging ESL students in the filmmaking process. Twenty-three undergraduate ESL students with linguistically and culturally diverse backgrounds in a large Canadian university participated in this project. Participants from 15 majors were randomly divided into five drama groups and contributed to the screenwriting, acting, production, and postproduction of a film.

The project outcomes show that filmmaking was a meaningful task which captivated students' imagination, enhanced their motivation, and facilitated their interaction with one another through compelling multimedia. More specifically, findings derived from observations, interviews, and corpus analysis indicate that filmmaking based on carefully written scripts, while at the same time allowing for personal interpretation of characters, is effective in creating an optimal learning environment for students' English acquisition, particularly in terms of vocabulary.

INTRODUCTION

Every year, 240,000 immigrants and refugees arrive in Canada, and approximately 130,000 international students enter the country to study (Citizenship and Immigration Canada, 2009; Statistics Canada, 2010, 2011). The majority

---

All the students' names in this chapter are pseudonyms.

of these students are nonnative English speakers who learn ESL. For instance, students from predominantly non–English-speaking countries, including China, India, South Korea, France, Saudi Arabia, Iran, Japan, and Nigeria, made up 92% of the international higher education students in Canada in 2010 (Institute of International Education, 2012). Research has shown that these undergraduate ESL students have difficulties with many aspects of learning in English-medium universities (e.g., Grayson, 2004, 2008, 2009). Grayson's (2004) study surveyed 5,830 students at York University, comparing the grade point averages (GPAs) of ESL students and their native-English-speaking Canadian-born counterparts. He found that the GPAs of newly arrived male ESL students were 20% lower than the male Canadian-born students. Female ESL students who had been in Canada since elementary school had an average GPA that was 11.4% lower than their Canadian-born counterparts. Grayson's further research on international and domestic ESL students at four Canadian universities (i.e., British Colombia, York, McGill, and Dalhousie) confirms that ESL students, independent of their domestic or international status, had difficulties in communicating with other students, reading course materials, writing reports or essays, and understanding course lectures (Grayson, 2008).

Research on both native language (L1) and second language (L2) acquisition has mostly attributed the challenges that students encounter in terms of academic performance to their failure in acquiring sufficient English vocabulary (August & Shanahan, 2006; Stahl & Nagy, 2006; Stanovich, 1986). According to corpus research, knowledge of approximately 3,000 high-frequency words significantly influences students' reading comprehension. This includes the 2,000 high-frequency words on the General Service List (West, 1953) that account for an average of 87% of a nonacademic text and 78% of an academic text (Nation, 2001). Adding 570 academic word families from Coxhead's (2000) Academic Word List increases the coverage of academic texts to 86% (Nation, 2001). Other proper nouns, technical vocabulary, and other low-frequency words account for the remaining 13% of words in a nonacademic text and nearly 14% of those in an academic text. For successful reading comprehension of a given text, research has widely recommended that students reach a minimum level of 95% vocabulary coverage (Nation, 2001).

In line with this corpus research, many studies and interventions have been conducted and developed to enhance elementary and secondary students' English vocabulary acquisition in the interest of improving their reading comprehension (e.g., Biemiller, 2008; Carlo, August, & Snow, 2005; Coxhead & Nation, 2001; Lively, Snow, & August, 2003; Nagy & Anderson, 1984). However, scant literature and resources are available that address the English vocabulary learning of ESL students enrolled in universities, particularly in the content-based classroom context. This chapter reports on a task-based language intervention that aimed at supporting the collaborative learning of English vocabulary among undergraduate English language learners (ELLs) when reading Canadian literature.

The intervention took the form of a filmmaking project in an undergraduate humanities course.

LITERATURE REVIEW

The use and production of videos by students has increasingly gained recognition for providing university and K–12 students with motivating and authentic learning experiences across disciplines (see, e.g., Gromik, 2008; Gross, 1998; Rubin, Bresnahan, & Ducas, 1996; Triggs & John, 2004). Several studies have shown that students in science and mathematics classrooms benefited from using and generating videos, because such activities enabled them to efficiently make observations, conduct research, collect data, and deliver presentations (e.g., Gross, 1998; Rubin et al., 1996). For example, Rubin and his colleagues (1996) studied how students used self-made videos to analyze motion sequences of their own body movements.

A number of articles have pointed out the promising potential of using videos for second and foreign language learning and instruction, especially online video clips, because the increasing capacity of the Internet provides learners with enriched and authentic language resources (Hanson-Smith, 2004). Video has become a popular medium for language teaching and learning as well as a self-assessment tool (Gardner, 1994). Language institutions, such as the National Association of Self-Instructional Language Programs, have dramatically increased the volume of Internet-delivered courseware which incorporates both audio and video components (Dunkel, Brill, & Kohl, 2002).

Some empirical evidence has also emerged from studies showing that digital video production in language classrooms can engage students in open-ended explorations in an authentic learning environment. Video production increases students' learning opportunities, supports their learning autonomy, and, most important, creates a contextual situation to help students develop cultural awareness. For example, Levy and Kennedy (2004) found that video recordings of the behavior of students studying Italian as a foreign language were effective in helping them visualize and subsequently correct their errors. When teaching a Multimedia English class to ELLs at a Japanese university, Gromik (2008) observed that video production supported by viable video editing software provided students with multiple opportunities to view and reflect on their use of English.

Research in vocabulary acquisition has also shown that the use and production of videos is more effective than other scaffolding means to support students' word retention. For example, Al-Seghayer's (2001) study shows that

> a video clip is more effective in teaching unknown vocabulary words than a still picture. Among the suggested factors that explain such a result are that video better builds a mental image, better creates curiosity leading to increased concentration, and embodies an advantageous combination of modalities (vivid or dynamic image, sound, and printed text). (p. 202)

Katchen, Morris, and Savova (2005) also found that video production activities allowed students to produce videos focusing on specific morphological and phonological forms of vocabulary items and enabled students to achieve better retention of these words.

To summarize, the literature in the field provides significant insights into the benefits of video use and production in language classrooms. However, limited evidence is available to support its pedagogical benefits for assisting ELLs in acquiring vocabulary. Further studies and interventions are needed to facilitate the application of video and digital media and to investigate the associated learning outcomes, particularly in content-based language classrooms (Hanson-Smith, 1997). In response to this gap in the literature, the present project invited students to "take ownership of the entire video production process" (Gromik, 2008, para. 7) in an attempt to enhance their learning experiences and their acquisition of vocabulary knowledge.

THEORETICAL FRAMEWORK

This project drew on the theory of task-based language learning and adopted its most recent conceptual framework, the third-generation task as defined by Ribé and Vidal (1993). This framework takes a more global perspective, with a focus on enriching students' personal experience. That is, the task or project must target not only the development of students' communicative skills and cognitive strategies required for real-life problem solving, but also the enhancement of students' motivation, creativity, awareness, and interpersonal skills. This enriched framework has been amply referenced and echoed by scholars in the field (e.g., Levy & Kennedy, 2004; Littlewood, 2003). Levy and Kennedy (2004) indicate that "learners need reflective activities to develop language awareness, as well as productive activities, in order to become effective and autonomous learners" (p. 53).

In sum, previous studies and theoretical frameworks inform the present project in terms of three salient aspects: (1) ESL students' vocabulary knowledge is a critical factor that determines their English reading comprehension and, furthermore, their overall English language acquisition; (2) the application of video, digital media, or both is an effective scaffolding approach to support ESL students' learning of many aspects of English, including vocabulary; and (3) a task-based approach has significant benefits for English learning through the transformation of ESL students' learning experiences. The present project adopted these theories and approaches to enhance ESL students' engagement with a work of Canadian literature and their learning of its related vocabulary through a filmmaking task.

THE FILMMAKING PROJECT

Context of the Project

The filmmaking project took place at a university in Toronto, Canada, among 23 undergraduate ESL students with linguistically and culturally diverse backgrounds. The participants represented 15 different majors, but all were registered in Introduction to Canadian Language and Culture, a 9-credit content-based course designed for both international and Canadian ESL students to allow them to fulfill their writing-intensive humanities requirement in a productive English for academic purposes (EAP) learning environment. This one-term "double-time" course that took place over the span of 15 weeks had the same number of contact hours as a yearlong course. The class met three times weekly, for a total of 8 hours a week.

The course focuses on fostering students' academic English skills and promoting students' awareness of multiple aspects of Canadian society and culture. It aims to embed language learning within programs on acculturation and citizenship. Over the years, it has evolved from being a largely literature-based course into one with scholarly articles focused on Canadian issues; however, the requirement of reading a novel remains a central component of the course. *The Edible Woman*, by Margaret Atwood (1969), the world-renowned Canadian author, was chosen on the basis of several features. First, it offers cultural content in an entertaining form. In a course focused largely on multicultural "new Canadian" viewpoints and experiences, this short novel explores the tensions within consumer culture, personal relationships, and individual choice and responsibility. It also provides students with a Canadian perspective, embodied in the characters of Marian and the supporting cast. The novel describes the historic downtown core of Toronto, where students can actually trace the paths that the characters take around landmarks such as the Park Plaza Bar and Queen's Park Circle. Published in 1969, this novel is also a document of early feminism, raising issues that feminists still struggle with. Most important, the book's action arises from universal questions that young people face when entering the adult world, such as: What will I do for a living? With whom will I live? Will I have children? What is worth doing and not doing in life?

The immediacy of these themes and settings can help students engage with the novel. However, grasping these important aspects of the story depends on other elements that threaten to completely escape L2 readers, namely, Margaret Atwood's mad-cap sense of humor and the quirky exploration of her themes, which are often rendered in graphic and figurative language. In fact, the outlandish vocabulary used in *The Edible Woman* is challenging for the very elements that are the strength of Atwood's novels. We both taught the course, and observed that due to difficult vocabulary items with culturally contextualized meanings in the novel, ESL students struggled to make sense of the plot and missed much of the action and humor of the book. They overlooked the curious and inventive imagery by which Atwood reveals the characters' often skewed points of view and the ironies and tensions of contemporary life—essential elements in the development of the themes of the novel. The students were often mystified by the explicit and bizarre nature of these images, and they tended to dismiss the novel as "weird." Students needed constant explanations to work through these vocabulary items. Only when they received such support could they understand culturally specific references and finally hope to understand, relate to, and even enjoy the novel. The filmmaking project aimed to alleviate the challenges presented by the novel's vocabulary, operationalizing it in a way that gave students access to Atwood's major themes.

Project Design

This filmmaking project intended to (1) optimize learning opportunities by engaging students in the multimodal learning involved in a full cycle of the filmmaking process, (2) motivate students' learning through drama activities that were of interest to them, (3) develop students' learning abilities by constructing a task-focused, collaborative learning environment, (4) encourage full participation of ESL students with different levels of language skills, and (5) enhance vocabulary acquisition through language output activities such as scriptwriting, drama performance, and intensive communication during film production. All of these aims served the ultimate goal of allowing the students to access the salient themes of the novel.

Student Participants

The project was conducted in the first author's classroom during her instructional hours for the course, Introduction to Canadian Language and Culture, from February to May 2009. Twenty-three ESL students with linguistically and culturally diverse backgrounds participated in the project (see Table 1). During class discussions, it was noted that many of these students had difficulty in comprehending the novel and lacked English vocabulary, including the first 3,000 words on the General Service List (West, 1953). For example, in one of the paragraphs of the novel, Lang said that out of 72 words there were 9 (12.5%) that he didn't know (see the bold unknown words in Figure 1).

Project Phases and Organizational Structure

The project consisted of two types of tasks: drama activities and film production activities. Hence, two categories of groups were formed: drama groups and production groups. Participation in the drama activities was compulsory; it counted for 15% of the final mark of the course. The students were randomly assigned to one of five drama groups to work collaboratively on joint tasks during class as well as outside of class voluntarily. These included reading and discussing the novel together, conducting research about its author and the historical and cultural

Table 1. Student Backgrounds

Students N = 23	Country of origin	Cultural background	First language
1	Afghanistan	Afghani	Pashtu
13	China	Chinese	Mandarin/Cantonese
1	Croatia	Croatian	Croatian
1	India	Indian	Urdu
1	Iran	Iranian	Persian
2	Italy	Italian	Italian
1	Pakistan	Pakistani	Urdu
1	Morocco	Moroccan	Arabic/French
2	Taiwan	Chinese	Mandarin

background of the novel, making decisions about plot and casting for the film, and negotiating different perspectives in interpreting characters.

One of the most difficult preproduction tasks was scriptwriting; it was a challenge for students to adapt the novel into different scenes with conversations that were informative, contextually appropriate, and interesting to the target audience, given their language proficiency constraints and the small size of each drama group (only four to six students). Students worked in groups to choose plot sequences from the novel for their scenes based on the requirements given by the instructor (the first author); the plot needed to (1) occur within a feasible

---

"Oh, one of those," Ainsley said, "They're such a **bore**." She stubbed out her cigarette in the grass.

"You know, I got the feeling that's why he's back," Clara said, with something like **vivacity**. "Some kind of a mess with a girl; like the one that made him go over in the first place."

"Ah," I said, not surprised.

Ainsley gave a little cry and **deposited** the baby on the lawn. "It's wet on my dress," she said **accusingly**.

"Well, they do, you know," said Clara. The baby began to howl, and I picked her up **gingerly** and handed her over to Clara. I was prepared to be helpful, but only up to a point.

Clara **joggled** the baby." Well, you **goddamned fire-hydrant**," she said **soothingly**. "You spouted on mummy's friend, didn't you? It'll wash out, Ainsley. But we didn't want to put rubber pants on you in all this heat, did we, you **stinking** little **geyser**? Never believe what they tell you about maternal **instinct**," she added **grimly** to us. "I don't see how anyone can love their children till they start to be human beings."

Figure 1. Sample of Unknown Words in an Excerpt of The Edible Woman

timeframe, (2) engage all group members, and (3) require enriched dialogues among characters. All groups consulted the instructor about their choices and received feedback before scriptwriting commenced. Students then submitted drafts of their scripts to the instructor for a second round of feedback in the form of editorial comments and overall suggestions for further improvement.

Production and postproduction groups were formed at the same time as the drama groups. Participants were recruited on a volunteer basis, and they were informed that their contribution in assisting production would not be counted toward course credit. Twenty positions for students were initially posted in the class, and 17 students actively participated in the production group. Three more positions were added upon the requests of students during the production and postproduction phases of the project. The instructor took on the roles of director and producer, providing students with guidance and coordinating activities at critical stages. The second author provided literary consultation for each drama group (see Table 2). Figure 2 demonstrates the different components of the project, comprising two lines of tasks: drama activities on the right-hand side and film production activities on the left-hand side.

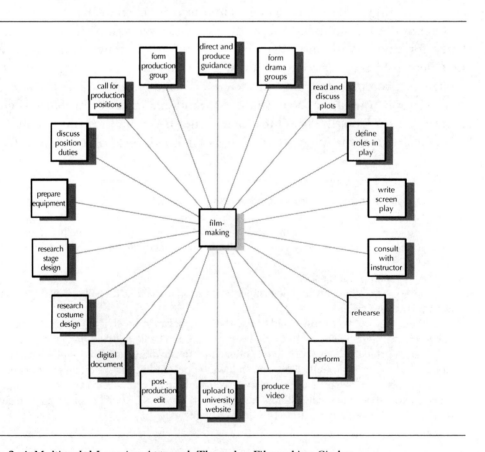

Figure 2. A Multimodal Learning Approach Through a Filmmaking Circle

Table 2. Positions for the Filmmaking Production Groups

Preproduction and production		Postproduction
*Director (1)	*Literary consultant (1)	*Producer (1)
Assistant director (1)	Assistant director (1)	Assistant producer (1)
Stage managers (2)	Stage coordinator (1)	Postproduction editors (stop-motion pictures) (4)
Master cinematographer (1)	Photographers (2)	Postproduction editors (video clips) (3)
Cinematographer (3)	Costume coordinator (1)	*Postproduction technical expert (2)
Makeup artists (2)	Stage technical expert (1)	*CD package designer (1)

Numbers in parentheses indicate number of students in each position.

*Positions taken by the instructors and external experts.

Equipment Access

Due to very limited access to university equipment, students and the instructor used their own equipment for production. This included one analog video camera, two digital video cameras, three digital photo cameras, a tripod, and seven laptop computers. Students felt that using their own equipment allowed them more flexibility during the production, and they were more familiar with this equipment. Even if there were any technical problems during class, they could always have the equipment with them and work on it at home or ask their peers for help during team meetings after class.

For stage design and props, the students and instructor also brought their own clothes, dolls, tablecloths, telephones, candles, fresh-cut flowers, empty beer bottles, glasses, bottles of water, and ash trays. Due to the limited memory capacity of the two digital video cameras, most videos were recorded with the analog video camera. However, this resulted in a labor-intensive task for the postproduction team, who had to convert the analog videotapes to digital MPEG2 and Windows Media Video (WMV) formats that were compatible with the iMovie program. During the conversion process, the team worked with an external technical expert and experimented with four different software programs.

Timelines for Production and Postproduction

The instructional period for reading *The Edible Woman* and preparing for video production started from the ninth week of the term. In the final week of the term, the students performed their plays in class and filmed their scenes. Due to students' timetable for final assignments and exams and the complication of converting the analog videotapes to the appropriate digital video format, the students edited their films after the class was completed. In July and August 2009, two postproduction editorial groups met. One group was responsible for editing stop-motion pictures, and the second group was responsible for editing video clips. Although students were given freedom to explore the different ways of film editing, the instructor hosted seven postproduction meetings with students to discuss the themes, presentations, and music selections for the film. The iMovie program appeared to be user-friendly, and students developed hands-on skills quickly, although they also indicated that some important features were not available and they believed that a more professional video editing program would be preferable.

Twenty-two students signed consent letters[1] giving permission to use their images in the noncommercial CD production and to upload the film on the university website upon the invitation of the department's EAP program coordinator. Producing and publishing their own film on the university website was perceived by the students as a notable achievement.

PROJECT OUTCOMES

Project Structures for Optimal Motivation and Efficient Collaboration

The project was divided into three phases, all of which involved complex, multifaceted activities (Levy & Kennedy, 2004). Its two-dimensional organization structure (i.e., drama and production groups) allowed students to have optimal opportunities to contribute to the project and interact with each other. Twenty out of 23 students (87%) in the class had one or two roles in both groups. For example, Mario played the character of Peter in his drama group, and he also volunteered as a stage manager, helping each drama group with stage design suited to their scenes. Carol played the role of Marian in the play with her drama teammates, and she also worked on the video camera crew as a postproduction editor. As the drama and production activities progressed in parallel, the project called for a wide range of skills and talents. Almost every student found his or her own niche in the production groups in addition to his or her role as an actor in the play.

Even recently arrived international ESL students who were initially quiet and hesitant to speak up in class became forthcoming and articulate in the early stages of the production. For example, Jian was a first-year student in computer science. He had arrived from China only 4 months before the course started. He always sat at the back of the classroom, and for almost 2 months he had never spoken up in class. Once the filmmaking project started, he gradually became a more active participant, and finally acted as an assistant producer for the project. He said the project enabled him to "find a way to participate in classroom activi-

---

[1] One student declined signing the consent letter for religious reasons, but she did actively participate in the project.

ties and communicate with other students." Most important, it helped him build self-confidence, as shown in the following transcribed conversation:

Instructor: I didn't know how to use iMovie at all at the beginning. I learned a lot from you. I almost felt it was easier and faster to learn from you guys than try to seek assistance from technical support staff in the university. Many of our students are really technology oriented.

Jian: Yes, these are applied technical skills. And they are not taught in university courses, so many students have more applied skills than their professors in the university, because you just have to spend a lot of time to try it out. Sometimes professors find themselves fixing one thing while another goes wrong elsewhere, but if you give such problems to students, they can fix it right away, because we have time . . . and had spent a lot of time on it. These are in fact just simple problems.

This project not only opened up multiple opportunities for students' active participation, but also encouraged students to form close bonds quickly in order to support intense coordination and interaction. For example, to achieve a thorough comprehension of the novel, students adopted jigsaw reading strategies, whereby each student was assigned a section of text to study in depth and report on it to the rest of the group. Such strategies were ideal ways for students to help each other cope with difficult words and unfamiliar expressions and had the added benefit of encouraging deeper interaction between students and the text. Students also conducted library and online research to understand and establish the essential personality traits of characters involved in their scenes. Each drama group self-organized after-class group meetings and engaged in discussions via instant messaging, email, and phone among themselves and with the instructor. The film project transformed a daunting reading task into enjoyable learning activities which enhanced students' motivation, creativity, peer support, and critical thinking. This is vividly displayed in Carol's words:

Instructor: I know our course was very intense. Within one term, we had to finish a 9-credit full-year course. There were a lot of readings and assignments. I'd like to know how you felt about the drama activities and film production.

Carol: To be honest, I didn't finish this book. But I . . . because of the drama, because we had the scenes like "in the bar, in Clara's house," I had to read more carefully and more specifically to know who the main characters are . . .

Instructor: So—[2]

Carol: So I got to know more. Because acting the characters in the book, I had to know the specific[s] about a character. I was acting as Marian, so I had to know more about her.

---

[2] Indicates utterance interrupted

Instructor:	You had to introduce—
Carol:	I had to introduce my interpretation of Marian to all the people. I just watched the stop-motion pictures, and knowing the background music, like, make me really missing those moments. (laughing)
Instructor:	Missing those moments of the performances? (laughing)
Carol:	Not only that day [we performed] because we have met like three times for this drama; it was really fun to discuss with them, to have the group work.
Instructor:	How did you feel about reading the novel?
Carol:	I really didn't finish. I cannot really . . . I didn't really know how to understand the characters before. I didn't know why she is doing this? Why she is doing that? It is really, the character is [///].[3] I couldn't understand the characters. It always . . . turned out to be boring after the middle part.
Instructor:	So . . .
Carol:	Yeah, because of the drama we had our focuses. During the practice, I was acting Marian like this. Jeena said, "No, Marian should be like this," and Elizabeth said, "No, Marian should be like this." You can see everybody has different ideas about Marian.
Lang:	Finally we agreed with each other.
Instructor:	Finally you agreed with one interpretation about Marian.
Carol:	The group work also made us close.

This project afforded students the opportunity to express themselves through the voices of the novel's characters and through their own much-needed digital video and computer technology skills. Students demonstrated unprecedented motivation in reading, discussion, and scriptwriting. The assignment required a minimum of one scene, but all five drama groups voluntarily wrote two to seven scenes (see Table 3). We regard this innovative instructional method as a promising alternative approach to teaching advanced-level Canadian literature to university ESL students. Drama-based filmmaking is profoundly different from the traditional instructional mode, because it integrates ESL students with different levels of language skills in creating an ongoing, interactive, and reflective learning environment.

Vocabulary Acquisition Through Productive Activities

Assessment of students' language skill development, including reading comprehension of the novel, was based on evaluations of their scripts and drama performances. On the day of videotaping their performances, students submitted their final version of the scripts to the instructor. Although students were not required to use specific words that originally appeared in the novel to write their scripts due to concerns that this might constrain students' creativity, they were encouraged to use new words they had learned during the class. A rubric was also devel-

---

[3] Indecipherable utterance

Table 3. Synopsis of Scenes by the Five Drama Groups

Scene	Group 1	Group 2	Group 3	Group 4	Group 5
1	In the bar	In the bar	At Marian's office	In the bar	On the subway (Marian and Ainsley go to visit Clara)
2	In the ladies' powder room	At Marian and Peter's house party	At Joe and Clara's house	On the street (when Marian runs away)	At Joe and Clara's front door
3			At Marian and Ainsley's apartment	At Len's house	Marian, Ainsley, and Clara in the backyard
4			In the bar	On the way home (Peter proposes to Marian)	Dinner with Joe and Clara
5				At Marian and Ainsley's apartment (discussing the baby issue)	At Marian and Ainsley's apartment
6					Marian and Len's phone conversation
7					Marian and Ainsley's conversation

oped to evaluate their performance, focusing on the extent to which students were (1) acting appropriately to their characters, (2) interpreting the plot and paraphrasing original descriptions and dialogues properly, and (3) being fluent in their dialogues and accurate in their word usage and pronunciation. These dimensions were clearly important, but vocabulary remained a major challenge for this group of ELLs in their efforts to master English language skills to the level required by the university. For this chapter, we focus on the discussions about students' learning of vocabulary.

Student feedback on the project confirmed our observations: Many undergraduate ESL students had difficulties in reading comprehension of *The Edible Woman* due to unknown vocabulary as well as the figurative use of common words in specific cultural contexts. In the following conversation, Kang indicated that he recognized less than 90% of the words in the novel. This is significantly lower than a minimum level of 95% of vocabulary knowledge, the threshold for comprehension of a given text suggested by Laufer and Nation (1999).

Instructor: How many words do you not know in the novel?

Kang: At least 10% of the words I don't know.

Instructor: You mean 10%?

Kang: Yes, over 10%.

Instructor: So it is a little bit too much [to comprehend the reading with such a high percentage of unknown words].

Kang: And I found there are a lot words [in the novel that] we don't really use in our conversation.

Instructor: Any other reasons . . .

Kang: Yes, yes, some words I know their meanings, but they seem to mean something else in the novel. I believe, about this point, ah (sighing) this is because of the culture, the cultural differences. You cannot even explain some words in Chinese. You must . . . , the meaning is different . . . even different. . . . They carry different meanings in different period of time.

Instructor: Yeah.

Kang: So it is hard to understand.

Scriptwriting in groups seemed effective for helping students develop in-depth understanding of the register of characters' utterances and word meanings in contexts. By working with their peers, students wrote up dialogues that were coherent with scene themes. They also provided clear stage directions for actors and scene-setting elements (see the Appendix). It was observed that during the performance, a few students were even able to improvise the dialogues appropriately without the benefit of scripts. This process stimulated the ESL students' language productivity and affirmed Swain's (1985) theory that comprehensible output is beneficial for the acquisition of new language forms. Swain indicates that when meaningful and purposeful activities require L2 learners to communicate a message to someone, they often make several attempts to achieve the goal by constantly reflecting and modifying their utterance, including pronunciation, word use, and grammatical forms. This significantly facilitates their learning in ways that differ from, but also complement, receptive language learning activities.

Using Cobb's (2006) Classic Vocabulary Profile version 3, we conducted a corpus analysis of students' scripts to examine their vocabulary coverage. The results show that the students' scripts, like the original novel, were nonacademic texts because percentages of academic words (0.71%–1.84%) were far below the 10% coverage typically found in an academic text (Nation, 2001). However, the results indicate that students used more complex vocabulary than an average nonacademic English text. With the exception of the scripts written by drama group 5, the first 2,000 high-frequency words accounted for only 80.32%–82.8% of the total words in all scripts, whereas low-frequency/difficult words (and a few proper nouns) accounted for 15.93%–17.83% of the words (see Table 4). With scripts composed of less than 87% high-frequency words (i.e., from the 2,000 most common words in English) and more than 13% low-frequency words, students

Table 4. Vocabulary Coverage of Screenplays by Five Drama Groups

Drama group	1–1,000 words	1,001–2,000 words	Academic words	Off-list words	Total words
1	73.71%	6.61%	1.84%	17.83%	1,301
2	77.37%	5.63%	1.07%	15.93%	1,971
3	75.49%	6.53%	0.73%	17.21%	2,313
4	76.17%	6.63%	0.69%	16.51%	2,895
5	84.42%	6.66%	0.71%	8.22%	1,983

Off-list words include technical words, proper nouns, and low-frequency words.

had created texts that were more sophisticated than an average nonacademic text (Nation, 2001). Observational evaluations of student performance using the rubric also suggest that they had sufficient comprehension of the vocabulary contained in their scripts.

Feedback obtained from the student interviews about this project was positive. Students said it was the project that nurtured their interest in reading *The Edible Woman*, which they initially found "difficult," having "nothing to do with their life," and "boring." The filmmaking activities integrated with drama performance helped them situate their learning within a real-life context. The incorporation of digital multimedia into the project helped to attract these modern, technologically savvy students and also provided them with many more collaborative and reflective learning opportunities than conventional drama activities would have. As a result, students indicated that they were confident discussing videotaping and film-editing techniques as well as sharing their own perspectives about the novel's themes, plot, and characters with their peers because they felt they could contribute to the project individually in their own distinct way. The students also expressed that making their own short film and presenting it to the faculty and other students of the university made them feel proud of themselves, which in turn, motivated them to work diligently. Overall, as measured by the classroom observation and preliminary assessment mentioned earlier, the students showed good progress in their reading comprehension and vocabulary knowledge.

CONCLUSIONS AND IMPLICATIONS

This filmmaking project embraced a framework of task-based language learning that focused on authentic tasks, integrated language and content, and involved all the aspects of the personalities of participants (Ribé & Vidal, 1993). It enabled students to establish a cohesive interaction structure in a meaningful context that captivated their imaginations and enhanced their motivation through compelling multimedia (Gromik, 2008, 2009a; Hanson-Smith, 2007). The outcomes indicate that filmmaking activities were effective in creating an optimal environment for students' English learning, due to the fact that they (1) allowed students to interface and experiment with digital technology; (2) attracted and integrated students into constructivist learning activities seamlessly; (3) were based on carefully written scripts, providing students with structure for the targeted language skills; (4) allowed for personal interpretation of characters, enabling students' creativity and furthering their enjoyment of learning; and (5) encouraged the dramatization of certain themes permeated with cultural content, reinforcing students' in-depth comprehension and critical thinking skills. As a result, students were able to develop an in-depth understanding of the novel and acquire vocabulary that was difficult for them to comprehend through traditional lectures, reading, and other regular classroom activities. Overall, the project highlighted the great potential of using digital video media and drama to facilitate students' English acquisition.

APPENDIX:
STUDENT SCRIPT SAMPLE BASED ON
MARGARET ATWOOD'S *THE EDIBLE WOMAN*

Home Party—Second Scene

Cast

Peter—Hang[4]
Marian—Nira
Ainsley—Elizabeth
Len—Chen
Clara—Jesamie

(Marian and Peter in the kitchen fix people drinks. The door opens and Marian begins to walk towards it. Clara and Len walked in through the door)[5]

Peter: How the hell are you? Good to see you here. God, I've been meaning to call you up.
(While Peter walks over to greet them, Marian feels nervous and freezes; not even saying "hi." Peter shakes hands with Len)

Len: OK, I guess. (nudges his shoulders)
(Marian grabs Clara by her coat sleeve and takes her into the bedroom)

Peter: Len let me get a drink for you.
(Peter and Len go into the kitchen)

---

[4] All the students' names are pseudonyms.
[5] Text in parentheses is stage direction.

Marian:	What is he doing here?
	(Clara takes off her coat)
Clara:	I hope you don't mind us bringing him, I didn't think you would because after all you are old friends, but really I thought we'd better; we didn't want him going off somewhere alone. As you can see, he's in piss poor shape. He turned up just after the baby-sitter got there and he looked really awful, he'd obviously had a lot. He told us an incoherent story about some woman he's been having trouble with, it sounded quite serious, and he said he was afraid to go back to the apartment, I don't know why; what could anybody do to him? So, poor thing, we are going to keep him up in that back room on the second floor. It's Arthur's room really, but I'm sure Len won't mind sharing. We both feel so sorry for him, what he needs is some nice home-loving type who'll take care of him; he doesn't seem to be able to cope at all . . .
Marian:	Did he say who she was?
Clara:	Why no, he doesn't usually tell the names.
Marian:	Anyways, come in. Let me fix you a drink.
	(Marian and Clara reached the living room and begin to talk)
Marian:	Why didn't Joe Come?
Clara:	Well, we weren't able to find a babysitter so Joe decided to stay home and babysit those devils. I was going to stay home with him but he insisted I go and pushed me out the door. He said, "go and enjoy yourself."
	(Behind Clara's back the door was opened and Ainsley came through)
Marian:	Oh, excuse me.
Ainsley:	Hi, sorry I'm later than I thought but I got this urge to start packing . . .
	(Marian hurried her into the bedroom)
Marian:	Ainsley, Len's here and I'm afraid he's drunk.
	(Ainsley looks into the mirror)
Ainsley:	Well, really Marian. It doesn't't matter to me in the least. After that talk this afternoon I'm sure we know where we stand and we can both behave like mature adults. There's nothing he could say now that could disturb me.
Marian:	But, he seems quite upset; that's what Clara says. Apparently he's gone to stay at their place. I saw him when he came in; he looks terrible; so I hope you won't say anything that could disturb him.
Ainsley:	There's no reason at all, why I should even talk to him?
	(Walk out of the bedroom)
Marian:	Stay here I'll get you a drink.
	(Marian went into the kitchen to get a drink for Ainsley and another one for herself. As Marian was going out of the kitchen she heard voices in the bedroom.)
Peter:	Hi honey, the party's really going! Almost picture-time!
Marian:	Here's your drink, Ainsley.
Ainsley:	Thanks.

	(Len stares at Ainsley. Ainsley smiles and is relaxed)
	(Marian's phone rings)
Marian:	Hello, hey Trevor. Oh, you guys won't be able to make it, not even Duncan . . . (pause).
Marian:	Can you give him the phone? Hey, why aren't you coming? But you have to, you have to meet Peter. I'd like you to, really, PLEASE.[6] Then where are you going? The Laundromat. Bye
Marian:	I can't face the crowded room again, but I have to.
	(Marian walks back into the living room and is behind Ainsley, and Len is in front of her)
	(Ainsley is whispering something to Len)
Len:	No, damn it! You will never get me . . .
Ainsley:	Alright then.
	(As Ainsley smashed her glass against the floor, the conversation stopped)
	(Marian jumps back)
Ainsley:	Len and I have a marvelous announcement to make (pause). We are going to have a baby.
Len:	You rotten bitch! (Says thickly but in a low voice).
	(Len smiles showing his teeth)
Len:	That's right, folks, and we're going to have the christening right now, in the midst of this friendly little gathering. Baptism in utero. I hereby name it after me.
	(Len grabs Ainsley by the shoulder and pours his beer onto her head)
	(Peter came charging in from the bedroom)
Peter:	Hold it! Great! That'll be a great one! Hey, this party's really getting off the ground!

---

[6]Tone emphasized

Challenging EFL Learners Through TV Advertising and Student-Produced Multimedia Projects

Joyce Cunningham

Using television (TV) advertisements involving well-known brand names and products can motivate and engage English language learners in active discussion in a collaborative learning environment. The Intercultural Communications course at Ibaraki University exposes Japanese English as a foreign language (EFL) undergraduates to advertising before undertaking a multimedia project based on making short TV commercials. In this way, the oral proficiency of these learners, who have had little or no contact with English-speaking countries, is improved along with awareness of persuasive advertising tactics. This chapter describes the two major challenges for students in this course: (1) using English actively to deconstruct advertisements and (2) incorporating advertising techniques into self-made digital commercials. The general procedure for making such video productions is outlined. Little research has been published on the effects of digital media on EFL students' oral proficiency and learning when exploiting advertising in the classroom. The present study seeks to answer the following questions: What is the impact of media production on students' learning of English, and to what extent can it increase their participation? How can current EFL pedagogical practices be improved when blending media with classroom language teaching? Student feedback is drawn from self-evaluations, interviews, and student logs in order to shed light on ways to enrich instruction, strengthen overall organization of course content, and increase students' learning.

Advertisements permeate the modern world and have a strong influence on our lives. One study found that U.S. "children view more than 40,000 commercials each year" (Wilcox et al., 2004, p. 4). Given this constant exposure, learning more about the persuasive intentions of advertising could provide stimulating practice to increase aural/oral English while raising students' awareness of the true significance of the brand names that they gravitate toward. As a teaching tool, short TV commercials are ideal for in-class activities and for analyzing cultural attitudes, beliefs, and behaviors. Speaking of pedagogy in the digital era, Nahachewsky and Begoray (2010) point out that "effective teachers are those who find a way to engage in new approaches by building on previous understandings" (p. 429). By engaging with students' background knowledge regarding their preferred brands and products, using commercials in the classroom can stimulate student interest and improve learning outcomes. It is also my belief that the project described in this chapter enhances not only language skills but also participation, motivation, problem solving, and critical thinking.

Although teachers generally support integrating technology into their English lessons to foster creative expression and critical thinking, actual practice appears to lag behind. In Japan, due to intense pressure from rigorous university entrance exams, there is little opportunity for pair or group discussion, and critical thinking is often discouraged in mainly teacher-centered classrooms that emphasize translation activities, rote learning, and memorization of vocabulary and grammar. In such contexts, educational technology use often takes the form of computer programs that drill students with more of these types of activities. For example, as Erkaya (2005) points out, students are not encouraged to share their points of view with their peers and teachers, whereas teachers are entitled to share their opinions with students, or even impose their opinions on the students. Thus, although studying a foreign language, some students do not identify with the target language or culture, and they often feel reluctant to speak if presented with the chance. However, when encouraged to collaborate on structured projects of real-world relevance, students often discover new strengths and talents within themselves while grappling with novel concepts and technological skills. Positive comments were received from students in the present project, such as from Makiko,[1] who said, "We learned about their culture. It was fun [and] . . . helped me to change different idea, information, viewpoint on commercials made by ourselves." These words clearly indicate that student experiences with such projects can foster new identities and a sense of pride in their achievements.

LITERATURE REVIEW

The use of authentic TV commercials has been researched and incorporated into effective language learning activities. Erkaya (2005) suggests techniques such as making predictions, brainstorming words or phrases that will be seen, using only the sound, transcribing the message, working with as many senses as possible to describe the commercial, and discussing the commercial from a prospective consumer's point of view. In addition, Schmidt (1998), Ambrose (2002), Sherman (2003), and Stempleski (1992) offer rich and varied activities but do not venture

---

[1]All student names in this chapter are pseudonyms.

solidly into the realm of film production or video editing in order to enhance the study of media literacy and improve language skills. Prior to the filming and video editing stages, it is useful to complete some preliminary activities. A general outline of such activities could include the following:

- screening TV commercials for applicability, appropriateness, and degree of interest for learners (e.g., fashion and brand names, cosmetics, sports)

- viewing and familiarizing students with TV commercials, their genre, and advertising techniques and claims

- developing learners' critical thinking by exploring how the advertiser makes the product more attractive or persuades the consumer to buy the product

- having students brainstorm and refine ideas for the final project while elaborating on and negotiating ideas with the instructor and student groups

Even with the huge strides being made in technology in recent years, teaching and learning practices related to filming and video editing continue to be largely overlooked, and practical information in this area is lacking. Some authors (e.g., Harris, 2006) do give extensive instructions to help teachers with preproduction, shooting, editing, and publishing procedures. However, these authors often do not attend to students' actual experiences when using digital equipment and editing programs. Fritsch (1998) describes simple, short, autonomous projects in which learners designed and produced vacation commercials on a single video camera, followed by viewing. Daniels (2004) mentions learner-generated video clips and proposes useful suggestions for filming and video editing, with students presenting their favorite restaurants, hometowns, or enjoyable activities. He recommends that teachers become familiar with video editing software. Nikitina (2011) describes a video project and analyzes the benefits for authentic language learning wherein collaboration leads to ownership of the learning. McGee and Fujita (2001) recommend preparing university EFL students for filming commercials by viewing "six commercials selling the same type of product . . . so that students are able to recognize different strategies used by makers of commercials to target certain groups of consumers within a given market" (p. 115). On another note, Yildiz (2008) reports on teacher candidates wishing to upgrade their knowledge of media and educational technology and integrate video production into their classes. This study highlights the importance for teachers of being aware of user-friendly video editing software before embarking on such a project.

Projects described by Henderson et al. (2010) and Kearney and Schuck (2004) refer to the learning that occurred through video production among elementary school students in Australia. The authors note that learning outcomes were principally those of communication, observation, and reflection, and pedagogy had shifted to a more student-centered approach, which also offered more opportunities for teachers to reflect on their practice. McGee and Fujita (2001) provide a practical master list of required vocabulary from the field of commercial advertising, along with helpful guidance for the teacher and students. Elsewhere, Concerned Children's Advertisers (n.d.) has supplied key terms and worksheets to increase awareness of advertising tactics, storyboards, and information about filming.

When using commercials in the classroom, it is critical to select commercials that are within the range of students' linguistic abilities and comprehension and are appropriate for the given age group. Commercials should contain simple language, everyday settings, and actions to which students can relate. Sherman (2003) advises the use of "images which suggest the product without revealing it . . . and an effective punch line, slogan or catchphrase" (p. 108). By careful selection, the teacher can settle on short, appealing, and dynamic clips that lend themselves well to classroom activities. The very brevity of these clips motivates students to watch them again and again, thereby improving listening skills. Moreover, the clips' accessibility via the Internet makes it easier for students to view them again on their own time, which would be helpful for students with lower proficiency. However, some content may be questionable, especially if assigned for homework. To avoid this problem, students can be invited to join a closed Facebook page where a choice of assigned commercials has already been posted.

CASE STUDY

The semester-long, 15-week course on commercials consists of 15 ninety-minute classes and is offered in the Intercultural Communications section in the Faculty of Humanities at Ibaraki University. Generally at an intermediate level, the participants have passed the Level 4 General Education English classes, with a TOEIC mean score of 551. Because the course is elective, each third-year university student must consider his or her objectives for attending these small classes. In 2009, only three students enrolled in the course, and in 2010, seven full-time students enrolled. In 2011, due to a scheduling conflict among other interested students, only one student enrolled. However, the insights and experiences gained from this sole case were most helpful, because there were fewer distractions and I had more time to interact on a deeper level. The course was divided into two parts. The first part consisted of exposure to advertising with careful scaffolding to build student understanding of its specialized vocabulary, claims[2] made by advertisements, and techniques used in producing commercials. The second part was the student-generated project itself. Please see the Appendix for a variety of course and project activities.

---

[2]The *advertising claims* (or simply *claims*) referred to in this chapter are techniques used by advertisers to inspire perceptions of the superiority of a given product.

To engage students actively in analyzing ads, I first elicited learners' most and least preferred commercials in their first language (L1). The students became the experts who explained the background, message, images, actions, and purposes of the commercials, while I took on the role of the learner. Another potentially effective technique here would be for small groups to make brief reenactments of such commercials; this technique has the additional benefit of helping students gain insights into the thinking of advertising companies and their commercials, which may have been viewed only passively prior to this time.

Two well-constructed PowerPoint presentations were particularly useful to introduce the essentials of advertising. These presentations give clear examples of advertising claims and techniques such as appeal to authority figures and ordinary people, snob and sex appeal, and the four Ps in advertisements (point of view, position, posture, and the person speaking). These presentations are titled "Recognizing Common Advertising Strategies" (Hatzigeourgiou, 2009) and "Advertising Techniques" (Nakazaki, 2011). Advertising notions from this material were integrated into classes to further familiarize students with TV commercials by showing examples of commercials,[3] which would reinforce the four Ps and general advertising techniques and claims from these two presentations. Prior to the project, the worksheet "Deconstructing an Advertisement" from Media Education Foundation (2005) provided excellent support for a more thorough analysis of such ads, which eased students into interpreting, evaluating, and analyzing them.

Given the sheer volume and the wide range in quality of available commercials on YouTube, a great deal of sifting through material was required to select appropriate commercials. All videos were previewed and selected based on appropriateness, vocabulary, pace, length, clarity of message, relevancy, and appealing content. To start with, the 1987 Diet Pepsi commercial "New Neighbor," starring Michael J. Fox (www.youtube.com/watch?v=zvsbeQbj8tM), was chosen for students to simply count how many times the product was mentioned. The commercial was short and full of challenges for the protagonist to face, and the ending was unpredictable. The well-chosen background music clearly demonstrated for students how music could contribute to the overall effect of the commercial. After viewing this commercial, students practiced with the transcript to infuse more drama, emotion, and voice projection into their own role-plays.

Homework for the project included weekly vocabulary logs and student journals, which engaged the class in learning and self-reflection. Journals enabled

---

[3]Among others, the following commercials (with purposes in parentheses) were used for this exercise: (a) Diet Pepsi (band wagon and sex appeal), as described in this chapter; (b) Visa (celebrity endorsement, explicit-implied message), http://www.youtube.com/watch?v=I4L1ut P35oA; (c) Seatbelt public service announcement (lends itself well to a storyboard exercise and example of public announcements), http://www.youtube.com/watch?v=t2o1oJ1zk_w; (d) Sapporo (position and point of view of product), http://www.youtube.com/watch?v=K-Rs6YEZAt8 &noredirect=1.

the teacher to become more aware of each group's progress and the difficulties that students encountered. Prompts were initially provided orally and on the blackboard to introduce the journaling activity. To foster more spontaneity and reflection in the log sheets, the rationale and general questions were explained as follows: "I am interested in your experiences, observations, learning, reactions, and feedback during this course. Please write at least half a page after each class and hand it in during the next class." The goal in the journaling activity was to encourage review of weekly activities as well as group work and to discuss impressions and insights that might not surface otherwise. Students were to focus especially on the learning in each class as well as what was interesting and surprising to them. They were to include individual or group challenges and problems during the activities, their feelings about these, and any solutions they found, as well as to mention questions and worries they might have. The vocabulary logs encouraged learners to take note of and write down words and sentences from a particular context to share in class. These scaffolds enabled students to describe the commercial with pertinent words in context.

PREPRODUCTION: RECORDING ROLE-PLAYS

Active practice is of utmost importance, and time on task can dramatically enhance learning and recall if students are more directly involved in an activity (Harris, 2006). Thus, role-plays preceded the actual filming and acting in the final video project and provided opportunities to discuss the results constructively. The goal was to keep role-plays as simple and familiar as possible while completing them rapidly. Thus, small groups focused on enacting a familiar family scene after deciding on family members, names, ages, jobs, and one family problem. They took brief notes, rehearsed briefly, and then filmed the role-plays. All students benefited from short appearances in front of a camera before the final project because some might have felt unprepared, reluctant, or anxious about being filmed. One student named Yoshiro, from the 2011 cohort, explained, "It was very shyness for me. Very hard for Japanese people to out [i.e., express outwardly] feelings but the commercial needs strong feelings. I must project feelings." These sentiments may be shared by many students in East Asian countries and can help the teacher understand why role-plays are an essential step in the project.

After watching the role-plays together, we focused on what students had done well to build confidence in risk-taking and creative experimentation. Finally, a goal-setting activity was assigned as homework to promote further self-reflection. A clear example of such self-reflection was provided by Sachiko, from the 2009 cohort, who wrote the following in her log after viewing her own role-play video:

> I should have performed more dramatically. I was very nervous so I couldn't talk
> a loud voice and perform very well. After we finished and watched it in the class, I
> regretted. I will try hard in the final video.

It is worth noting that activities involving video production warrant careful consideration by practitioners. For example, implementing these activities with large groups of students would be more challenging, as the number of video cameras has a direct impact on filming schedules. In such cases, some students should practice their role-plays while others are filming. Time should also be allocated for viewing and discussing common errors such as filming into the light or turning backs to the cameras. Some other points that should be covered in the context of these role-play videos are body language, eye contact, intonation, loudness, and the general effectiveness of the role-plays.

Once the class had viewed several commercials and attempted a first film appearance, students found a topic suitable to produce as a commercial for their final project. In groups, students brainstormed products they used and liked and then agreed on a message, slogan, and technique or claim. The San Diego County Office of Education (2009) advises that "each team 'pitch' their product . . . [to] check idea feasibility and be certain that the video plan has been thought through" (p. 4). Strong planning created more successful products, and having an evaluator assess the feasibility of students' ideas and provide constructive feedback about the strengths and weaknesses of the project assisted in refining their plans. In addition, the pitch was a valuable opportunity for students to build enthusiasm for the project, use voice projection and appropriate body language, and incorporate some drama into their explanation. Students could write down ideas on large sheets of white paper in text or picture form. Each member took a turn at explaining the product, title, message, and technique or claim. By organizing one idea per page and posting them on the walls, learners could better articulate their goals and develop their plans. In this way, all members were able to visualize and work on the organization of their pitch at once. Students were instructed to refer only to the notes on the posted papers.

A normal TV commercial lasts from 30 seconds to more than 1 minute, and it was therefore required that scripts not exceed 2 minutes in length. One enormous benefit of shorter scenes and dialogues was that students were under less pressure to memorize. However, creating dialogues took time, and approximately two class periods were required. It was acceptable for students to loosely base ideas on real TV commercials. The focus was less on narration and voiceover, and more on group interaction when writing active dialogue for each scene, wherein all members except the director of a particular scene appeared and spoke. Before dress rehearsals, scripts were practiced.

After scripting the dialogues, each group focused on designing a storyboard, the project blueprint that included outlines and sketches of information such as settings and props. Storyboards served as road maps, which encouraged the planning of ideas scene by scene, as well as locations, camera positions or angles, the shots, and the approximate length of each scene. The San Diego County Board of Education's (2012) *Production Tips,* which supplies sample storyboards and worksheets, could also be used as a resource for creating storyboards. Storyboards helped students break down scenes into the shortest units possible. This had a huge impact during filming, because longer scenes took time and effort to reshoot. Dress rehearsals were essential to check on the flow and energy of each scene and address technical issues such as forgotten props, pronunciation, facial expressions, and gestures. Meanwhile, the individual directors of each scene also practiced with the camera in place to check the positions of actors and products as well as to experiment with different camera angles. Finally, prior to filming, students signed a release form (Glass, 1992).

Production Process

The digital aspects of student-generated commercials were created in two stages: filming and editing. Of course, filming went more smoothly when students had prepared well. This meant that locations for filming had been verified and storyboards had been reordered and adjusted to reflect conditions such as lighting, space for the camera, and the framing of each scene. In her final self-report, Yuka, from the 2010 cohort, realized the importance of the setting: "Our camera angle had to be changed because just filming at the front angle is boring. Different angle makes audience attract[ed] more [to the product]."

Although student preparation is crucial to success, there are also many practical things teachers themselves can do to ensure smooth preparation and organization during the video production process. The importance of respecting time slots when working with the cameras and computers should be impressed upon the students, and in doing so, they will learn time management. Sign-up sheets for camera equipment should be posted in accessible areas. A checklist of basic equipment required for filming can be distributed so that nothing is missing before heading out:

- newly charged camera batteries and a charger in case of emergency
- a head set
- a video tape (if needed)
- an external handheld microphone with fresh batteries
- a tripod
- and so on

There should be a safe place to keep the group video when not in use so that a late or absent classmate does not cause undue stress when failing to appear with the tape. Effective camera use should have been explained previously (e.g., framing for camera angles, different kinds of shots, shooting extra blank footage before and after each scene). Finally, the instructor should be available and reachable while students are shooting during class and after, for problems crop up and some creative solutions may be suddenly needed. I took these practical steps in the present case study, and it greatly complemented students' own efforts.

This activity further extended students' technical literacy in terms of both audiovisual recording equipment and digital video editing software. For filming, a tripod and microphone were needed; the tripod keeps the camera steadier to facilitate video editing afterward, and the microphone improves audio quality. We used Apple iMovie 2 and iMovie 11 for all digital video editing purposes. The newer version of the program (iMovie 11) had various user-friendly features that enabled students to produce higher quality videos. For example, the new audio editor can modify voices to sound like they are on radios or telephones, and the pitch can be made higher or lower. If there is unexpected background noise, original footage can be muted and newly selected music or sound added. Special effects such as slow motion or fast forward are also easier to apply to the clips. To this end, a student named Satomi wrote in her group evaluation, "Setsuko said to me 'We have to use it. Tempo is very important point of commercial! In this case, slow is bad!' . . . Simple commercial is boring." On the newer version of iMovie, files can also be saved much more readily to a number of social networking sites such as Facebook and YouTube or synced with iTunes.

It was important to celebrate the successes of students who appeared in front of the camera, used computer video editing software, and cooperated in groups to respect deadlines while producing creative video clips. The commercials were then viewed by an exchange class at the University of Alabama at Birmingham (UAB). Students in this exchange class were eager and curious to watch and did so without judgment. After each viewing, the UAB students were encouraged to ask questions, and one or two constructive points were written by all and redistributed to each group in the original Japanese class. The exchange class procedures are described in more detail next.

EXCHANGE CLASS AND PROJECT ASSESSMENT

A real target audience outside the country heightened interest, engagement, and motivation, although identifying partners required time and effort. Through an exchange class program, the class in Japan received input from native-speaker peers rather than from the teacher or classmates. The students at UAB who were our partners for the present project were unexpected because they were studying Japanese, not English.

I was able to forward our 2011 production videos directly via Dropbox, a free online service that allows users to upload and share files from anywhere in the world. The UAB class viewed and evaluated the 2011 clip according to various criteria, including originality, effective slogans and messages, the use of at least one or two advertising techniques or claims, background music, and camera work. Written comments by UAB students were emailed to the class in Japan, and the videos were also discussed between the two classes via Skype. In order for interaction to be more meaningful for the target audience, Yoshiro prepared as both director and actor to answer questions and explain behind-the-scenes decisions and challenges. To build on his linguistic and cultural knowledge, he wanted to understand his U.S. audience's perceptions of the commercial and its potential effectiveness in the United States. Comments from UAB students were constructive and positive; they included specific information about his oral English abilities (e.g., intonation, pauses), which he particularly appreciated.

In this project, work was collected in various ways for assessment purposes. First, understanding was evaluated through more traditional means, such as several short vocabulary quizzes and a test on advertising claims and techniques. Second, summative weekly journals tracked individual effort and gave insights into students' learning processes. Third, vocabulary logs were completed by students. And finally, portfolios of work were compiled throughout the course. These portfolios included examples of work in progress on video production as well as final self-reflections on the challenges and problems encountered when working individually and in groups. Printouts were made of the questionnaire, storyboard, dialogue, personal assessment of the group's video clip, and a final self-evaluation along with the grade the student believed he or she should receive. These assessment strategies helped students develop metacognitive skills and assisted them in becoming more self-directed in their learning. Finally, teacher observations of class work, filming, and video editing provided further reference for assessment.

CASE ANALYSIS OF YOSHIRO AND HIS PEERS

It is essential that EFL learners who share a native language receive opportunities to practice speaking English with each other. In the context of this particular project, increasing oral expression during group work was crucial, because there was a tendency to lapse into Japanese during group activities when brainstorming or grappling with sophisticated technical terms or software. In working with Yoshiro, the only student enrolled in the 2011 class, I gained valuable insights. He was highly motivated and determined to take full advantage of the class to improve his English. He felt he lacked vocabulary as well as confidence in expressing himself orally, and he especially wanted to improve these areas. Yoshiro's opinions about his speaking skills concurred with students from previous years' classes; he also admitted to having little or no video editing experience and knowledge of media literacy. Because dialogue is an essential component in each production, Yoshiro invited another Japanese student, Wataru, to perform with him. This gave Yoshiro valuable opportunities to use his spoken English with a fellow speaker of Japanese.

For his project, Yoshiro decided to create a commercial about the energy drink Red Bull. He chose this product due to his own reliance on energy drinks to stay awake to finish his final essays at the last minute. Thus, he chose his topic based on his own experiences and background knowledge. The commercial Yoshiro created featured himself consuming the product and becoming rejuvenated in order to complete last-minute academic tasks. Like students from previous classes, Yoshiro used only words he was comfortable with, which were also easier for him to say and remember. Past groups had made commercials about a Japanese hot pot, a delicious snack, and a visit to a traditional Japanese home.

Although Yoshiro confessed to a general dislike of school assignments, he managed well with the video project and completed the editing on his own time. His positive attitude is clearly demonstrated in his journal:

> I was interested in using iMovie. I haven't used it . . . and it was the first time with computer editing, so I was very worried. It is a nice feeling to finish my big work so I felt to get big success.

As mentioned by Henderson et al. (2010), "the process of digital video production and most importantly, the process of reflection, allow[s] students to find their own pathways in learning, while still engaging with the key curriculum goals" (p. 16). This was certainly the case with Yoshiro; in truth, it was the first time in the history of this class that a student had completed the video editing outside of class without assistance. Yoshiro showed evidence of problem-solving skills, which allowed him to excel at this task. For instance, uploading and integrating appropriate music to iMovie 11 was a challenge for him initially; however, Yoshiro displayed his increasing autonomy by searching the manual and even visiting a media professor for advice.

Yoshiro's journal revealed some doubts about the purpose of the video editing project. He wrote, "To use iMovie 11 is to know about editing way rather than to improve my English." He had a valid point, and I interviewed him to search for solutions together. We considered lengthening the video editing period, but we came to the conclusion that such a modification was not feasible due to scheduling difficulties. Rather, Yoshiro suggested that the initial period dedicated to advertising techniques be shortened. In this way, more time could be spent on the project itself. Yoshiro explained:

> Before making the commercial, I watched a lot of commercials. It is nice for Japanese people . . . [who] haven't watched [foreign] commercials. . . . But if you shorten the [initial example] commercials, and give students [only] two to three [advertising] techniques, maybe it is enough to understand. . . . If there is more time, they can remake some scenes . . . there will be more time for editing. . . . There was no time, so I couldn't do it.

Following his suggestions, the final class sessions could be used to review and consolidate advertising techniques while viewing more commercials. Students often speak mostly in their L1 when contending with highly technical vocabulary and concepts during the editing process. To increase English speaking practice, we therefore decided that during each class of video editing every group should report orally to the instructor on planned or completed work. Moreover, in order to simplify the editing period, the instructor or an assistant could do certain basic, time-consuming, or mechanical tasks such as importing group clips into the computers, inserting the music, saving files, exporting and uploading the finished video, and making copies for students. This would allow students more class time to discuss advertising.

By sharing commercials with native speaker audiences, Yoshiro hoped to increase his oral communication skills and improve his speaking confidence. He willingly attended the extra Skype session at the end of the project so that UAB students could comment on the commercials. His confidence seemed to improve, for he stated,

> It was the first time to use a web camera. The last time I had a chance to talk to an Alabama student . . . we [didn't have a] webcam. It was very hard because I couldn't see him, his body language. But today, with the picture it helps my English. And they were always smiling so I can feel comfortable to speak.

Yoshiro also appreciated the additional opportunity for direct communication:

> It was most useful information for me. I was lucky to spend time to listen their impressions. It was a nice chance to practice my listening and speaking skill[s]. I feel [the UAB students] are very smart. I learned English for 6 years, but it was examination English. They are learning communicative Japanese."

This realization was crucial in that it strengthened Yoshiro's determination to actively practice English. He and I also understood how important webcams were as a visual aid to comprehension.

Tim Cook, the UAB professor of Japanese who was involved in the exchange classes, reported about the video project as follows:

> I have been able to give my students numerous opportunities to interact with their peers in Japan, both in Japanese and in English. . . . Attendance was voluntary and 11 turned up for the viewing. Students viewed the video 30 minutes prior to the Skype call and students watched the commercial with an eye for critiquing it later. The producer-actor in the commercial, a male student with a flair for acting, gave a humorous performance in which the advertised energy drink gave him super energy, as he signified through fast motion video and upbeat music. My students laughed throughout and asked to watch again. Representative comments were mostly about the actor, such as "He's funny" and "He gets the point across." They also thought the use of fast-motion video was effective in conveying his newfound energy from the drink. To improve the video, they made comments on the produc-tion decisions. While they liked the fun upbeat music used for energetic work, students thought that an even faster beat might have been more effective. They would have also worked on some of the actor's English. While they found his Japa-nese accent charming, they would have corrected his misplaced emphasis on certain words and choice of wording here and there. However, these were minor issues. While they enjoyed the video, even more exciting was talking directly with the star himself. They continued talking about favorite music, free time activities, and other topics typical of young people everywhere, sometimes in English and sometimes in Japanese, and were excited to find common interests. Many asked for the Japanese student's Skype address.

With the permission of all involved, the 2011 Ibaraki-UAB Skype session was videotaped so that Yoshiro could review and reflect more deeply on the information contained within—U.S. verbal and nonverbal communication, in particular, facial expressions and body language. In his final evaluation of the project, Yoshiro expressed satisfaction and enhanced confidence: "This event was very delightful for me because I could communicate [with] foreigner."

Yoshiro's awareness of advertising strategies also increased over the course of the project. In his words, "Always before, I just watched commercials. I don't think about [them]. After I learned the techniques . . . when I watched commercials, I think, 'Now maybe they are using this [advertising] claim or that claim.'" Sachiko also showed proof of critical thinking in her observations of the project in 2009: "I could learn how commercial is made and how important to think about what the company wants to say to persuade people." Other students from previous classes highlighted the positive outcomes of the video project. For instance, Kana wrote, "It was a fantastic experience to make our own commercial. . . . I thought it was difficult to make film smoothly and naturally but in fact, I enjoyed editing: for example I enjoyed choosing music and putting [effects] on film."

It was fascinating to follow and observe Yoshiro closely, and I felt we were co-constructing the commercial and learning together. In effect, I became his assistant director; the position of the product and camera angle became important to me as his success and his learning became my success and my learning. I had time to think about what he said or wrote and received good ideas for improving my pedagogy. In the process, Yoshiro was gaining more practice in communicating his preferences to me.

CONCLUSION

The present project yields some valuable insights into TESOL practices that integrate digital video production into the curriculum. First of all, teachers must be aware of issues that can arise during the course of a video production project such as the one described in this chapter. For instance, starting with a lower risk activity such as role-plays lessens student apprehension by providing a series of specific steps and guidelines and creating an opportunity for success before the final project. Second, although the initial brainstorming and video editing stages can take a great deal of class time, these steps are crucial to the process and are well worth the effort. In my experience with this course, students often worked very efficiently to complete these tasks during class time, because it was quite difficult to hold group meetings outside of class due to scheduling conflicts. Upon further reflection on the 2011 class, it would have been useful for Yoshiro to work more on his pronunciation and rhythm with members of the exchange class. In a language class, a native speaker instructor may become so adept at guessing student pronunciation and intonation that she or he fails to catch errors a foreign audience may not understand, which was exactly what happened in the 2011 production. More time for communication with the exchange class will certainly be integrated into the course in the future.

During this student-centered course and hands-on project, active communication skills were nurtured through discussion and evaluation of authentic advertising concepts and through the production of commercials for a real international audience. Learners were required to express themselves verbally when working in groups to brainstorm, write and revise their scripts, negotiate messages and slogans, organize settings and props, and integrate claims and techniques from the advertising media. As Foss, Carney, McDonald, and Rooks (2007) note, "in a world in which cooperative group efforts and achievement of tangible products is often a measure of success and accomplishment, project-based learning prepares students well for real world events" ("Final Thoughts"). Students in the present case study collaborated on a variety of activities, employing the real-life skills of acting, filming, video editing, and time management. They learned to assess their own and others' work through portfolios and were finally able to actively express themselves with confidence in authentic interactions with international peers.

As Pearlman (2011) states,

> students of today enter an increasingly globalized world in which technology plays a vital role. They must be good communicators, as well as great collaborators. The new work environment requires responsibility and self-management, as well as interpersonal and project-management skills that demand teamwork and leadership. (para. 8)

It is my hope that this project challenged students to develop just such skills—and also to become more aware of the consumer society in which they live and critically analyze some of the implicit messages and slick images of advertising.

ENDNOTE

Teachers should be aware of copyright laws. Erkaya (2005) states, "In America, if used for educational purposes and where no fees are involved, it may be acceptable. Concerned instructors should verify the regulations but, if worried, . . . use for one semester and then change." Brant (2005) also adds, "Screenrights—The Audio-Visual Copyright Society does however make it possible for schools, TAFES and universities to use such material for educational purposes by entering into an agreement. As a result of this agreement, institutions are given permission to copy programmes from radio or television (both pay and free to air). More information can be found at (www.screen.org) or by emailing the company (licensing@screen.org)." Copyright laws are tightening, so copyright clearance on free social media sites such as Flickr or Picasa are helpful for self-created material.

APPENDIX:
COURSE SCHEDULE

Week 1   Course introduction. View student-generated commercial. Start print media commercials with "Recognizing Common Advertising strategies." Homework: Write down two to three products for final project.

Week 2   Discuss favorite TV commercials. Teach "Advertising techniques." View and analyze TV commercial.

Week 3   View TV commercial. Introduce role-plays for next class. Brainstorm product. Form groups. Homework: Test on advertising strategies.

Week 4   Sell group commercial to teacher. View another class-made commercial. Work on role-plays. Advertising strategies test.

Week 5   Film role-plays. View and discuss constructively. Begin work on final project: Brainstorm ideas/details.

Week 6   View TV commercial. Work on dialogues.

Week 7   View TV commercial. Finish work on dialogues.

Week 8   Begin storyboards. View another TV commercial. Introduce iMovie.

Week 9   Finish storyboards. Dress rehearsals: When ready, practice in front of instructor, and film parts of project. Skype with exchange group.

Week 10 Finish dress rehearsals. Continue filming.

Week 11 Start video editing.

Week 12 Continue video editing.

Week 13 Finish video editing. Send to exchange partners.

Week 14 Whole-class viewing of final projects presented via panels of directors. If time, work on portfolios. View another commercial.

Week 15 Skype with exchange partners for feedback on videos. Finalize portfolios. Course wrap-up.

CHAPTER 8

Female Arab Students' Production of Cell Phone Videos to Enhance English Skills

Nicolas Gromik

Conducted at Qatar University, this case study reports on undergraduate female Arab students' use of the cell phone as a tool to enhance their English language abilities and discusses their perceptions of the educational benefits of using the cell phone video recording feature. The project was conducted over the course of 1 month as part of an academic writing course. Eight female students volunteered to participate in the research and to produce videos with their cell phones. Due to students' cultural tradition, the videos were evaluated only by the teacher and were not uploaded in the public domain. The evidence collected reveals that project-based activities were most suitable for these English as a foreign language (EFL) learners.

LITERATURE REVIEW

Cell phone technology includes a wide range of functions. It enables people to send text messages, play games, record voices or make short videos, take pictures, listen to music, and access the Internet anywhere and anytime at their convenience. Cell phones are used every day for various reasons in different contexts and are considered a necessary, personal appendage. The devices are also user-friendly tools that do not require a great deal of knowledge to operate. The potential educational benefits of cell phones have been receiving increasing attention from researchers, but these benefits have only been partially explored.

Cell phones have been used in educational settings in Australia, Japan, and Taiwan for the purpose of exposing language learners to vocabulary items via text message (e.g., Kennedy & Levy, 2008; Lu, 2008; Stockwell, 2010). Another cell phone feature that has received research interest is the camera. In Japan, Okabe and Ito (2003) investigated the relationship between photo storage on cell phones and personal identity creation. Since then, research from various countries has contributed to a wider interpretation of the connection between cell phone photos, people's lives, and knowledge acquisition. In another study,

Italian youth were observed to use their cell phone cameras to document their lives and surroundings (Scifo, 2009). Research from China reports that taking photos with a cell phone has become a common phenomenon and the technology helps individuals capture and store memorable events; the visual cues provided by photos help them interpret, reflect on, and participate in their world (Gai, 2009). One basic conclusion reached by the aforementioned researchers is that cell phone cameras are utilized to define personal realities.

In a study conducted at a university in Cyprus, the cell phone camera was successfully integrated into a project aimed at developing undergraduates' awareness of environmental issues. Uzunboylu, Cavus, and Ercag (2009) explain that "students used mobile telephones to photograph local subjects, which included environmental blights and social events" (p. 384). The researchers received and organized the photos on the project's website, and students accessed that site to view and comment on the photos submitted by their peers. Responses revealed that "students learned to value mobile technologies and their use for reporting and sharing these problems by facing environmental problems in real time" (p. 385). Uzunboylu et al.'s research reveals that students could use their cell phones to take on the more authentic project of documenting environmental pollution in their town in order to learn more about the targeted content. This suggests that the cell phone camera has great potential to engage students in a better understanding of their academic courses by completing project-based research.

A more recent development than the basic camera feature, cell phone video capture has received relatively little research attention. In a blended learning experiment conducted at a Japanese university, I engaged students in producing cell phone video diaries to be stored on Blip (http://blip.tv), a video storage website. Seven advanced EFL learners used their cell phones to video record their thoughts and opinions about various topics of personal relevance (Gromik, 2009b). For example, one student made a video of a dinner with his family at an ethnic restaurant. Another explained her daily bicycle ride to university. The students created one cell phone video per week and managed a subscriber's account on Blip. On this site they wrote why these particular videos were important to them. The project revealed that students were able to use technology to share video files and make short English explanations of their daily activities with their peers. By uploading their videos online, they were able to share real content with peers, who in turn, could comment on their videos and stories. It became possible to use these online texts and videos in the classroom to discuss authentic content, which engaged students to become more inquisitive about their daily lives. The learning outcome was that students used the technology to improve their ability to discuss authentic experiences in English.

Given the opportunities that the various cell phone features afford, the present research reports on a project aimed at encouraging female Arab students to use the video recording feature on their cell phones to document the use of technology in their studies and daily lives. Its objectives were to determine

(1) whether this group of students was willing and able to produce cell phone videos on a given theme and (2) whether video production could assist them in enhancing their English skills.

THEORETICAL FRAMEWORK

In order to facilitate educators' understanding of EFL learners, Cummins (1984) identifies a developmental distinction between conversational and academic communicative skills: basic interpersonal communication skills (BICS) refers to learners' conversational fluency in a language, whereas cognitive academic language proficiency (CALP) refers to their ability to express concepts and ideas relevant for academic discussion. Not all students are proficient to the extent of participating in academic conversations. Chamot and O'Malley (1987) explain that as students progress with their education, they experience increases in academic rigor and expectations. Referring to Cummins's work, it seems that participants in the Academic Writing 2 course at Qatar University possessed BICS to a sufficient degree. They had adequate listening and speaking skills to conduct everyday conversations about topics of a nonacademic nature. However, these students did not possess sufficient CALP necessary to engage in the kind of academic tasks required by the course. Cummins also suggests a framework in which students can be involved in either cognitively demanding or undemanding tasks depending on their abilities, and that tasks can be either context embedded or context reduced. Whereas in context-reduced activities there are few if any cues to guide students' performance, context-embedded activities give students the chance to use audiovisual cues to assist them with the production of a task.

Table 1 lists the types of tasks that teachers can require students to complete (Cummins, 1984; Chamot & O'Malley, 1987). Based on my teaching experiences and observations in both Japan and Qatar, typical speaking classes in these contexts provide ample opportunities for students to engage in context-embedded and context-reduced tasks of an undemanding nature. However, few courses challenge students with demanding tasks.

Table 1. Examples of Tasks

	Undemanding tasks	**Demanding tasks**
Context embedded	• Playing communicative games • Engaging in face-to-face interaction	• Making academic presentations with visuals • Making brief oral presentations
Context reduced	• Participating in predictable conversation	• Delivering formal speeches without visuals

Source: Adapted from Chamot & O'Malley (1987).

By encouraging students to use the video recording feature on their cell phones, it was hypothesized that students would be capable of shifting from undemanding context-embedded and context-reduced tasks to demanding context-embedded tasks on their own.

Project-Based Learning

Research suggests that a project-based learning method is effective to help students learn about course content (Uzunboylu et al., 2008) and to improve their understanding of a target language (Gromik, 2009b). This method engages students to cooperate with peers in order to undertake a challenging authentic task. Project-based learning also requires learners to choose the process for completing the task. Once the project is complete, not only have students gained or consolidated certain skills, but the project itself also has provided evidence of the new skills they have acquired and how much they have improved at communicating their opinions and ideas (Lam, Cheng, & Choy, 2010).

CONTEXT, PARTICIPANTS, AND METHOD

The Academic Writing 2 course was divided into two parts. The first part exposed students to academic writing. During this phase, students in small groups wrote a short academic paper on a theme provided in the textbook. During the second part of the term, students formulated a research question based on their individual majors. Because the second part of the course was more flexible and students had gained some appreciation of the writing process, I decided to introduce the cell phone project at this stage.

At Qatar University (n.d.), 77% of the student population is female. This gender ratio and segregated classes provided an opportunity to understand specifically how female Arab students could experiment with cell phone video recording technology to improve their English skills. Seventy-five students enrolled in the Academic Writing 2 course that I taught in the spring of 2011. All participants in the course were female, and they came from various areas in the Persian Gulf region. These students had either achieved a 5.5 or higher IELTS score or successfully completed all the English Foundation Program prerequisite courses.

In the second half of the semester, all students enrolled in the course were encouraged to volunteer for the project. Eight students agreed to participate. Although all participants were competent cell phone users and a few had previously made videos with digital video cameras, they were not familiar with the video recording feature on their cell phones. All were familiar with their phone's traditional camera feature.

Cultural traditions stipulated that some of the students in the study should not show photos of themselves to males or over the Internet. In addition, depending on their cultural heritage or religious influence, some female students at Qatar University wear a Maghreb (face covering) and do not show their faces in public.

These cultural and traditional values are not at the center of this research, which focuses primarily on the processes and strategies that students used to create videos and ultimately enhance their academic English skills. However, because cultural heritage had a strong influence on some students' use of image and video recording technology in the present study, the inclusion of this aspect was warranted in the interest of gaining a more complete understanding of this group of students.

The eight volunteer students were each required to make one 30-second movie in English per week for 4 weeks using the video recording feature on their cell phones. Although the small sample size could be considered a limitation, the focus of this research is to document students' perceptions of the educational benefit of using the cell phone as a learning tool.

The project theme required students to discuss and document examples of technology integration in their surroundings. This task was deemed appropriate because it was within students' academic and conceptual reach and is highly relevant to everyday life in the modern age. Students were not required to upload their videos online. Students sent the videos directly to me, and I then provided some face-to-face or email feedback on their performances. Students were informed that the project was not a tested task and they would not receive a grade. However, I would be able to give them advice on possible strategies to improve their English and filming skills as well as the content of their videos.

As previously discussed, students enrolled in the Academic Writing 2 course can typically express themselves on general topics (i.e., BICS), but they have difficulty explaining more abstract ideas or discussing academic issues in depth (i.e., CALP; Cummins, 1983, 1984). The participants in the present study also fit this description. The content of the videos was therefore analyzed in terms of their use of CALP in tasks that were both cognitively demanding and context embedded.

The first set of evidence collected was the cell phone video recordings. Students emailed their videos directly to my work email account. In addition, students were encouraged to send a brief written explanation of their video production process. Finally, interviews were conducted with all participants to discuss their progress, concerns, and opinions of the task.

VIDEO RECORDINGS OF PARTICIPANTS

Eight students were asked to submit four videos each. Of 32 potential cell phone video recordings, the students submitted 21 videos in total. Three students submitted all four videos, and one student did not submit any videos. Among the remaining four students, one student submitted one video, one submitted two audio files, one submitted two videos, and another submitted three videos. Table 2 provides an overview of the content students discussed in their videos and the filming location.

Table 2. Summary and Location of Students' Video and Audio Content

Participant	Format	Content	Setting
1	Video	• Viewing the university website on phone	• At home
2	Audio	• Examples of cell phones as distractions • Tools accessible on cell phones	• At home, background classical music
3	Video	• Using WhatsApp for broadcasting • Using Facebook to chat with friends	• In library
4	Video	• Using YouTube to study accounting • iPhone task manager app • Using the Internet to access the university website	• At home • On campus
5	Video	• Using cell phone in history class • Using iPhone during class a distraction • Report on cell phone addiction • Two boys in restaurant playing iPhone games	• History class • At home • In restaurant
6	Video	• Useful cell phone features • Useful iPhone apps to study • Using cell phones for entertainment • Using text-chat for homework	• In cafeteria • In empty classroom • In empty computer laboratory
7	Video	• Using calendar feature instead of diary • Using photo feature instead of scanning • Using Facebook to communicate with peers • Accessing the university website on cell phone	• In library • At home • In cafeteria

Participant 1

This participant returned one video out of four. She reported no specific constraints apart from being unable to find content that demonstrated the integration of technology in everyday events. In her video, the student explored the possibility of viewing the university website on her phone. The video was produced at her home, and it showed the cell phone screen and the university website. She navigated through the website to show some of the challenges of viewing web content on a cell phone. The video was well structured, and the student's explanation was clear and to the point. However, her narration included some grammatical and syntactical errors. During the interview, the student commented that she had written a script, which she read out loud. It was her first time hearing herself speak in English, and this was an embarrassing moment because she had thought that her pronunciation was better than it actually was. She understood that the project could help her improve speaking without notes, but she was not sure how to develop speaking strategies to improve her academic speaking skills.

Participant 2

Instead of sending in videos, this participant submitted two audio recordings. In the first audio file, she discussed the disadvantages of using cell phones, identifying them as distractors and devices that are frowned upon by parents. In the second audio file, she continued to discuss the use of cell phones, focusing on personal uses of the tool. Reflecting on her own experience, she commented that at times her cell phone was not helpful because its small screen was not suitable for accessing the Internet. In both recordings, the audio was clear and the student used classical music in the background. However, based on her speed, intonation, and pauses while speaking, it was deduced that this student was reading from her notes rather than speaking without any prompts. In the second recording, she used more sentence transition key words, indicating again that she had written a speech. During the interview the student revealed that she had written a script and read from it. She explained that producing a script gave her more confidence about her speaking ability.

Participant 3

Although this participant produced two videos, both were recordings of her voice with minimal visual cues for two reasons: She did not feel comfortable showing her face, and she felt it was easier to operate the video recording feature by placing the microphone closer to her mouth.

Both videos demonstrated cell phone application use, and both were recorded in the library. In the first video, the student explained her use of WhatsApp, a text-based app for sharing information with peers. The video was a brief demonstration of broadcasting. The screen only revealed the students' list of friends with whom she broadcasts information. This participant did not read from a script; instead, she relied on the process of WhatsApp broadcasting to produce her speech. There was a brief introduction and conclusion, but the speech was informal in structure.

The second video was fairly similar to the first in structure. The student opened Facebook on her cell phone and then explained the process for chatting. As in her previous video, this video also included a brief and informal introduction and conclusion. Because the video was a live demonstration, there were brief moments of silence, so the student did not make the most of the recording time to speak. This participant was very enthusiastic about the project. During the interview she mentioned that although preparing a speech was challenging, video recording her thoughts was a great concept, and she planned to use this technique in the future to document her family life.

Participant 4

For this participant, the project offered a new way of learning and evaluating her English abilities. The first video captured her navigating through YouTube to search for videos that discussed accounting. The footage showed one main video, and then the student discussed the various videos on the side of the screen. Although the audio of YouTube video was rather unintelligible, the student's voice was clear. The student's speech followed the following structure: self-introduction, introduction of discussion topic, discussion of content available on YouTube, benefits of using YouTube to learn, and conclusion.

The second video was filmed in an empty classroom, and the student was assisted by a friend. The student sat at a desk and demonstrated the iPhone app Errand (which helps to plan daily activities) on her phone. Only her hands and the cell phone were displayed. Unlike the first video there was no introduction; instead, she began her description of the app immediately. She finished the speech with a brief conclusion explaining that because she had so much to do at university, this easy-to-use app helped her manage her time better. The vocabulary used in the video was simple and at times repetitive.

This participant's final video was filmed at her home. She explored the university website and explained the benefits of the university email feature. The footage revealed the process she used to access her email, keep in touch with other students, and store university administration messages. In this video there was a brief introduction explaining the need to check email anywhere, anytime. There was a brief explanation of the benefits of the university email account for storing different types of email, and the conclusion identified WiFi as a beneficial service for accessing the Internet to read university email. During the main body of the speech, the student lost focus a bit and began to explain the various benefits of WiFi. This suggests that she was speaking spontaneously and made use of the visual cues to bring the speech back on track prior to the conclusion.

It was evident that during the production of the first video this student was not certain of the benefits of using the cell phone video recording feature to practice speaking in English. However, upon viewing her first video, she understood that the video itself revealed her speaking ability. She realized that if she could remember the overall presentation structure, then she could also remember the sentence format for introducing a topic and concluding a speech.

Participant 5

This student created videos that reflected on her use of technology in her daily activities. The first of her videos was about her use of her cell phone during a history lecture. She was not paying attention in class; instead she was playing and texting on her cell phone. The speech in this video was a discussion identifying the reasons why she was playing with her phone. There was no conclusion, and the student's final statement was off focus and grammatically incorrect.

The student's second video explained why she was not paying attention in class and how the cell phone had distracted her. Based on a comparison of her speech performance in the two videos, it is evident that although this student's first video was more spontaneous, she wrote a script and practiced her speech before producing the second video. There was a clear introduction that identified her reason for not paying attention in class, followed by an example of the type of cell phone feature that caused the distraction. The conclusion suggested that students could put texting notices on silent mode.

This participant then followed up on her idea of the cell phone as a distraction and created a third video discussing phone addiction. The video camera recorded what seemed to be the student's *abaya* (traditional long black dress) while she explained why she thought many students are addicted to using cell phones. Similar to the second video, the structure of the presentation in this video revealed that the student had written a script and practiced her speech beforehand. The introduction and conclusion were clearly marked with key words. The body of the speech included sentence transition words as well as short topic sentences to describe two main phone addictions.

The fourth video showed two young Qatari boys sitting at a restaurant with their cell phones in hand. The student explained what she was observing, commenting that the two boys, although sitting at the same table, were not talking with each other. The video was filmed in a restaurant, but there was minimal background noise interference. For this video the student was unable to write a script, so she gave a spontaneous speech. Nonetheless, the speech in the video indicated that she had spent some time thinking about the issue she wanted to cover in this video. There was a clear introduction regarding phone addiction. The main focus of the presentation was the two boys' lack of communication with each other, and the conclusion referred back to the larger issue: phones as a distraction.

In all four videos the student's voice was clear, and there was minimal background noise. Furthermore, the student used a structured format to express her opinions succinctly, demonstrating the development of critical academic language skills (i.e., CALP).

This student was very positive about the project during the interview. She explained that the video recording helped her think about an issue before she began discussing it. She also noted the need to reflect on the best strategy to sound convincing about the issues she addressed, something she had not thought about before. "I simply spoke," she pointed out, but now "I think before I speak."

Participant 6

This participant had made family videos in the past, and she had edited and stored the movies on her computer but did not upload them to the Internet. She thought that the cell phone project was a great idea, but she soon realized that making videos in public places could be problematic. She tried to make a video in the library but was told to be quiet. When she tried to make her video in a coffee shop, conversations of other patrons created too much background noise. She was finally able to record her first video in the cafeteria and the remaining three videos in empty classrooms.

This student's first video was a demonstration of the use of an Arabic-English translation app. Her second video reviewed two apps that could be used to study. In the third video, the student reported on the problems with her cell phone keyboard. The final video was a demonstration of iMessages, an iPhone app that offers free texting between two iPhones or iPads. The student used two phones for this demonstration. In all of her videos, she had assistance from a friend who acted as the videographer.

Similar to previous participants, this student's speech structure provided evidence that she had written a script; all of her speeches included an introduction, a main story or problem, and a conclusion. However, due to strong first language influence, I initially presumed that she was speaking spontaneously. During the interview, this participant explained that she had written a script but that she had not been able to memorize it verbatim so she made some mistakes. This led her to rely more on her prior knowledge of the language and visual cues to remember her speech, which can be seen as evidence of her ability to complete this context-embedded demanding task.

Participant 7

This student had already experimented with most of the features on her cell phone except the video recording feature. She also commented that she used her phone for educational purposes, such as taking notes or using Skype to talk to her peers about school-related topics during class breaks. This student also had prior experience producing family videos with a digital camera. Like the other participants, she had not posted any of her videos online.

The first video she created for the project was rather simple in structure and content. She explained the use of the calendar feature on her phone. She showed her diary and then explained the process and benefits of transferring the information contained in it onto her cell phone. Although the introduction and the explanations were clear and the idea flowed smoothly, the student had difficulty with the conclusion. No visual cues were available, so she had difficulties remembering this part of the speech. As a result, the conclusion had longer pauses and some repetition.

In the second video, the participant explained the process and benefits of using the cell phone's traditional camera feature to take pictures of her class notes to send to a friend. Although this was a practical and unscripted video, it lacked structure. It began with a strong introduction that identified the benefits of using the camera feature to photograph and email notes. However, once this had been explained and demonstrated in the body of the speech, the student still had 5 seconds left to speak and it was apparent that she was not prepared for this. Instead of a conclusion, she decided to identify another benefit of this feature, the fact that it was free, but then abruptly ran out of time.

The third video showed the student's class Facebook page, where one of her professors uploaded questions for students to answer. Demonstrating improvement over the student's two previous attempts, this video had a clear introduction and conclusion. The main story was divided into three parts: the lecturer's reason for using Facebook, student access to all the posts, and the possibility to network with peers. The vocabulary used was not extensive, but the whole speech demonstrated the student's ability to deliver a speech with limited visual cues (i.e., a demanding task set in a context-reduced scenario).

The student's fourth video discussed the benefits of accessing the university website on a cell phone. Similar to her third video, this video had a clear introduction to identify the purpose of the speech. The body of the speech explained the three challenges of using the university website on a cell phone. The conclusion stated that these challenges were caused by limitations in cell phone technology rather than the website itself. The student's voice was clear, the content was specific to the issue, and the speech included transition key words and sentences. In this video the speaker was clearly able to demonstrate her ability to deliver a more formal presentation with effective visual cues.

This student was so enthusiastic about the project that she met with me several times to discuss each topic she wanted to address. During these discussions, it became clear that she wanted to produce short professional videos about specific issues regarding cell phone technology. I also noted that although she did not have any major challenges with expressing her opinion, she still needed to focus on addressing the issue without getting distracted, which often happened during our discussions. She commented that the time limit set by the cell phone recording feature was a motivating factor to keep her on task.

LEARNING OUTCOMES

One of the objectives of the Academic Writing 2 course is to teach the importance of using structure in academic writing, particularly with a focus on learning to include an introduction, supporting body paragraphs, and a conclusion. The project provided students with the opportunity to confirm and reinforce their knowledge learned in the academic writing course and to apply their ability to express their ideas and opinions in a more academic format with or without visual cues.

The following is a sample that provides a good example of such structure being used in an oral presentation:

> In this video, I will talk about the problems of the keyboards of cell phones. Although the developments of cell phones have tried to make the keyboard bigger

than before, it is still small and the keys are attached in a way so people make mistakes while they are typing. Also as you can see, each button contains more than a letter. They have many symbols such as numbers and Arabic script and many things that make people find the keyboard complicated to use for learning purposes.

In the speech sample, the student began with an introduction focusing on the problems she had identified. She then shifted to the main points of her argument. And she finished her speech with a cause-and-effect statement.

Six out of eight students wrote either a full script or some key words related to the topic they wanted to discuss in advance of their video productions. All of these students explained that they hoped to improve either their speaking speed or their pronunciation.

Participants 4 and 7 did not write scripts or notes. Both of these students indicated that their majors were a motivating factor in their decision not to use written notes. Participant 4, an international affairs major, commented that although speaking without notes led to more errors, she perceived the need to redo the videos as beneficial to learning. On the other hand, Participant 7, a mass communications major, was able to speak spontaneously because she had prepared herself. Not only had she practiced speaking faster, but she also had practiced using the technology before video recording herself demonstrating its use, and she used the editing software available with her video recording feature.

All seven students practiced their first speech three to ten times before achieving a suitable performance. The amount of practice was reduced as students gained more experience with video production and speech preparation. The evidence collected from Participants 4 and 7 suggests that through the project they were able to successfully perform demanding context-embedded tasks. These two students also demonstrated an ability to shift from using the everyday conversational structures characteristic of BICS to a more structured speaking format that demonstrated CALP.

Regarding video production, all students indicated that even after practicing their speeches, they still made some errors during the recordings. These errors were usually due to unsatisfactory pronunciation or forgetting the content of their speeches. However, by the third and fourth videos, students commented that because of the practice and experience with video production, they were able to develop effective strategies for remembering the content of their speeches. As one student explained during an interview:

> In my first video I was not sure what I wanted to say. In the last video I knew what the main point of my video was. I knew what I wanted to say. Instead of focusing on the words I had written in my script, I focused on the purpose of my video, and this helped me use the right words.

The cell phone video recording feature empowered students to self-evaluate their performances before sending their final videos to me. The video performances were a visual reminder that motivated students to reconsider their speaking abilities. As one student explained:

> After making a video I evaluate myself. I imagine myself as the teacher and I think about the comments the teacher might make. For example "why is she humming, or using that word?" or "why is she using that position of the camera?" When I hear my voice I think it is not a professional speech, and I don't pronounce my words very clearly. So I make a new video to improve my pronunciation.

Because the students were able to record their videos many times, they took the initiative to correct the grammatical structure of their speeches before turning in their final videos. Aside from pronunciation, the only obvious difficulty was the selection of appropriate words, an element of academic language that could be further developed through teacher feedback on the videos.

STUDENT ATTITUDES AND PERCEPTIONS

One participant produced audio files only. Of the remaining six students, who submitted videos, only two students showed their faces on their videos. The remaining four students focused the video camera lens on the visual artifact in discussion. During the interview, the audio-only student explained her reason for choosing to make audio recordings:

> I decided to do audio recordings because in our tradition or culture it is not popular to do videos because of the rules girls have to follow. Many years ago it was not allowed to do audios. Now girls can record their voice because you do not see the face, so for girls it is acceptable. Girls and boys aren't allowed to be together. For me it is not acceptable.

Another student concurred with that statement and added during her interview that the focus was on the object, not her:

> I didn't want to show my face because the topic is about the use of technology, so I wanted to show technology. Also I cannot show my face, even if the viewer is my teacher, so I had to find a way to show something.

A third student commented on the physical structure of the cell phone as a reason for not showing her face in her video. She explained that because of the video lens location on the phone, opposite in direction to the microphone, it was not possible to show her face and record her voice with high quality.

All students perceived some educational or personal benefits from producing videos with their cell phones. As explained previously, some female Arab students are not allowed to show their faces in public. Therefore, some of the participants' parents wanted to preview the videos. For two students, this was helpful because their parents were the first critics of their final videos, and these students received assistance with the content production. Some parents offered their opinions of technology use in their lives. Also, showing the videos to their parents built trust between parent and child. One student commented that her father did not view the last video because he trusted the production process and visual content.

Showing the videos to their parents and the self-evaluation process combined to create a positive experience for students. Not only did their parents' support give them confidence, but the whole preparation process reassured them that the task was achievable. Although all students commented on being nervous in their first videos, those who went on to produce a third and fourth video agreed that they had the confidence to speak in English because they had practiced expressing their opinions or presenting technical explanations many times.

All participants recommended this project to become part of the learning process in future English programs. They believed that creating cell phone videos assisted them in understanding the writing process as well as improving their speaking abilities. Two students commented that the main obstacles to including this learning method in university courses would be parental consent and university policies. Although Qatar University launched its mobile website in early 2012, cell phones are still banned in the classroom.

LIMITATIONS

The production of cell phone videos was not without limitations. Most students commented that the cell phone screen was too small to view their videos. One student decided to email herself the videos so she could view them on her computer screen.

The most challenging part of the video production was finding an appropriate recording location. As can be seen in Table 2, students attempted to record their videos in public spaces such as the university library. Students who used these spaces commented that they were inappropriate due to the background noise created by other students talking. The solution was to find empty classrooms or locations that were not in use. Some participants made their video recordings in the cafeteria at times when most students were in class.

One of the eight participants did not submit any videos. She was invited for an interview in an effort to understand her reasons for not completing the project. She commented that making the cell phone videos in addition to writing an academic paper for the course was demanding, and she did not think she would have enough time. She also pointed out that the quality of her cell phone video camera was not good enough to undertake the project:

> This is probably a lame excuse, but my cell phone camera is not that great. It's not very clear for videos and photos (although photos are better). The other reason [is] my phone memory is not big. I can have around two videos at max. I don't use my cell phone camera for videos and rarely do for photos.

This student's comment illustrates the simple but formidable limitation presented by the technology itself. In order to utilize cell phone video production for educational purposes, all participating students must possess cell phones with the necessary capabilities. Rapid advances in technology will undoubtedly lead to more cell phones equipped with more advanced video recording features, but it is still unlikely that every student in a given class will possess such a phone.

DISCUSSION

As stated earlier, the objectives of the present study were to understand (1) whether or not female Arab students would be able to use the video recording feature available on their cell phone to produce English videos and (2) whether the technology would assist them in enhancing their English skills.

Seven out of eight participants were willing and able to partially or entirely complete the project. The constraints that some students who did not fully complete the project experienced were not due to the task itself, but rather to external factors that prevented them from completing it. These factors included other course requirements and cell phone limitations such as poor video recording quality.

For participants who did not express any concerns or constraints, the task was manageable and within reach of their linguistic abilities and content knowledge. Because they were in control of the speech production, many students wrote scripts or were able to use key words as guidelines, and some were eventually able to speak more spontaneously than they had anticipated. The students were able to create video resources that clearly addressed the assigned focus. The topics covered were varied and revealed that students were able to reflect on their use of technology using structured, academic discourse. The time limit set by the video recording feature did not prevent students from explaining their opinions clearly and to the point.

Video production was a revealing task for some of the students. It enabled them to hear their voices for the first time. Although some students stated that they had delivered public speeches in the past, they had never had a chance to view or hear their own performances in English. The experience motivated them to improve their pronunciation and academic language skills. Some students explained that they were more careful with the words they chose to use in their videos. In fact, a few admitted to avoiding more challenging words because they were difficult to pronounce accurately. This runs counter to the notion that the task encouraged the development of CALP, but it is worth noting that structural elements of academic discourse were frequently demonstrated in students' videos. For some students, the task was more meaningful because they considered the project an opportunity to produce an audiovisual broadcast that was relevant to their studies.

As noted previously, the participants in the present study possessed the BICS necessary to conduct daily discussions, but they often struggled with CALP. The video project revealed that students generally made efforts to shift from a BICS style of communication to a CALP style in order to deliver technical explanations and express their opinions. The task of giving an oral presentation on technology use was a cognitively demanding one, requiring careful topic selection and structure according to academic writing principles. In addition, the visual elements in the videos provided a context in which these verbal presentations were embedded. In other words, the video project provided students with a series of demanding context-embedded tasks. The immediately available video evidence afforded students the opportunity to view and reflect on the quality of their productions.

Overall, the participants enjoyed producing videos with their cell phones and were able to perceive some educational benefits from completing the task. Students who wrote a script and practiced more extensively provided more complete and detailed opinions on their video topics. These students clearly achieved gains in their oral English proficiency. The project also encouraged some students to speak more spontaneously and to think about the benefits of using the cell phone video recording feature as a learning tool.

CONCLUSION

In contrast to the bulky and expensive video cameras of the past, cell phones are compact devices that are relatively inexpensive and enable their users to become independent producers of video content on a variety of topics. As technology develops, cell phones and their video cameras will continue to offer greater audio and visual recording capabilities. As students become more familiar with digital video cameras and the editing process, cell phone cameras could provide them with greater mobility to record events in various settings that relate to personal and academic interests as well as issues covered in class. Using the video recording feature on their phones can also provide students with greater opportunities to express their opinions more confidently.

It is worth noting that the preliminary findings reported here cannot be generalized across the whole female Arab population. Further investigation of female Arab students' use of cell phones and video production for learning purposes is warranted. In addition, further investigation of the impact of traditional culture on video production among the Arab community is necessary to better understand the constraints that female students face and design similar projects that can be duplicated in other educational settings. However, the present research provides a useful example from which educators can draw as they begin to explore the cell phone video camera as an educational tool.

As female Arab students continue to gain support from their parents and communities to express themselves on camera, they may be able to produce video documentation that further demonstrates the educational benefits of using technology in their daily lives. As the participants in this study explained, it was not possible in the past for female students to record their voices. However, most of the participants were able to use the video recording feature while finding methods to comply with their cultural and traditional values.

The present research also has implications that reach beyond the Arab world. The fact that all participants in this study were able to successfully employ academic English discourse structures in their videos is particularly promising, because it suggests that such video production activities may assist students in one of the most challenging tasks facing language learners—the development of what Cummins (1984) identifies as CALP. As such, English language educators across contexts should consider engaging students in the production of cell phone videos, particularly in conjunction with a project-based learning methodology that involves content discussions.

CHAPTER 9

Video as an Instructional Tool for ESL Learners in the United States: A Review of Previous Research

Nicholas Edwards, Jingjing Jiang, Peizhao Li, and Jia Li

The rise of digital technology has provided many new opportunities for language teaching and learning. Digital video is of particular interest to the field of teaching English as a second language (ESL) due to its capacity to present oral language in a variety of authentic contexts. This chapter reviews the research literature on the use of digital video as an educational medium for ESL learners in the United States. The reviewed research suggests that digital video can have a positive impact on various language learning outcomes for this population. Video that is rich in contextual information or is presented with English captions may be particularly beneficial for improving learners' language skills. However, the findings of much of the current research are limited by methodological constraints such as cross-sectional designs, small sample sizes, and qualitative self-report measures. Furthermore, the vast majority of the research is done on adult college students and may not generalize to all populations of ESL learners in the United States. We therefore conclude that more large-scale, longitudinal research with quantitative measures is needed to further clarify the nature of the relationship between specific instructional uses of digital video and language learning outcomes. Implications of digital video research for practitioners are discussed, and directions for future research in this area are suggested.

As the pace of globalization quickens, immigrants and students from around the world continue to pour into the United States for a host of personal, professional, and educational reasons. As a result, the demand for ESL education in the United States is higher than ever before. At the same time, the rise of digital video and multimedia technology presents exciting new opportunities for ESL learners. Video allows language to be embedded in more authentic contexts than are possible through the mediums of audio or text. Through video, situational and cultural information can be vividly presented in both verbal and nonverbal ways that are accessible to language learners. Furthermore, there is mounting evidence that the presentation of information through both auditory and visual channels can improve memory formation and retention (e.g., Rose & Dalton, 2009).

As the use of video continues to increase in language classrooms and digital language learning environments, many questions about how to most effectively use video as an instructional tool have also arisen. In response, researchers have increasingly explored ways in which audiovisual technology can be used to teach nonnative languages over the last decade (Vanderplank, 2010). Although much of this research has taken place in other countries, the present review focuses on studies conducted in the United States. The research reviewed suggests that digital video can have a positive impact on motivation and language learning outcomes for ESL students; videos that are rich in contextual information and are presented with English captions may be particularly beneficial. However, more research is clearly needed to determine the nature of the relationship between specific instructional uses of digital video and language learning outcomes.

LITERATURE SEARCH METHOD

Articles were found via searches of three online databases: EBSCO Academic Search Premier, ERIC, and Education Abstracts International. The search term *digital video* was alternately entered in all possible combinations with the terms *ESL, EFL, EAL, ELL, ESOL, English, language learn*, English learn**, and *English teach**.[1] Because the present study was concerned with all forms of video (not just digital), the term *digital video* was shortened to *video,* and all nine searches were repeated. Finally, all nine terms were entered alternately with the term *CALL*.[2] In total, 27 searches of each database were conducted. All empirical studies examining the use and production of digital video for the purposes of ESL learning and teaching were included, regardless of age or nationality of the participants or the nationality of the researcher(s), as long as they were conducted in the United States. Studies using qualitative and/or quantitative measures were included, regardless of specific methodology or year of publication. Studies that were not conducted in the United States or did not specifically examine ESL teaching and learning practices that made use of digital video were excluded, as were studies that dealt with the learning of languages other than English. Although studies examining the use of video production as a pedagogical tool were within the original scope of the review, no such studies were found that met the other criteria for inclusion. The present review thus focuses solely on the viewing of video for the purposes of ESL learning and teaching. Altogether, 12 articles met the criteria for inclusion.

---

[1] ESL = English as a second language, EFL = English as a foreign language, EAL = English as an additional language, ELL = English language learner, ESOL = English to speakers of other languages.
[2] CALL = computer-assisted language learning.

VIDEO AND LANGUAGE LEARNING OUTCOMES

The use of video has been examined in terms of various language learning outcomes, and video shows promise as an educational medium for increasing the receptive language skills of listening comprehension, reading comprehension, and vocabulary acquisition as well as fluency in both oral and written language production. Findings relating to each of these domains are discussed in this section.

Listening Comprehension

Overall, the reviewed literature suggests that the use of video as an instructional tool can be effective for improving adult ESL students' English listening comprehension (LC). According to Wagner (2010), video has been increasingly used in the second language classroom for the cultivation of listening comprehension in recent decades due to the common belief that the inclusion of nonverbal elements of the spoken texts will enable listeners to better understand their content. Wagner's study examined the effects of "videotexts"—short video clips of both mini-lectures and dialogues that ranged from 1.5 to 4 minutes long—on the LC outcomes of adult ESL students ($N = 202$) enrolled in a community English program. All participants were exposed to the same series of videotexts and answered several written multiple-choice LC questions after each mini-lecture or dialogue in the series. Classroom groups were randomly placed into video + audio or audio-only (video screen covered) conditions. Results show that the video groups performed significantly better than the audio-only groups on LC test questions for both genres of videotext. To account for this difference in performance, Wagner hypothesizes that the video scaffolded comprehension through both (1) environmental information, such as the setting and the number of people present, and (2) nonverbal communicative cues, such as gestures and body language.

Wagner's (2007, 2008) earlier studies using the same videotexts and pool of participants shed light on learners' videotext viewing behavior. In the 2007 study, individual participants ($N = 36$) varied widely in how much they looked at the video screen, though as a group they looked at the screen significantly more for dialogues than mini-lectures. Wagner attributes this to the more engaging nature of the dialogue videos and to the fact that they contained more useful nonverbal information relevant to the test questions. Furthermore, there was no difference between screen viewing behavior toward the beginning or end of each video, or between earlier and later videos in the series, indicating that participants did not find the visual input to be a distraction. Wagner's 2008 study employed think-aloud procedures with eight participants of advanced proficiency levels to determine what nonverbal aspects of the videotexts learners were attending to and using in their responses to LC test questions. Participants varied widely in both their abilities to (1) attend to the nonverbal cues in a video and (2) use these cues to correctly answer test questions.

Based on the results of these three studies, Wagner (2007, 2008, 2010) argues that nonverbal visual information should be included in definitions of listening comprehension. With the exception of talking on the phone and listening to the radio, real-life communication situations require a language learner to simultaneously use verbal and nonverbal information to understand the speaker's meaning. Thus, the variance observed in learners' viewing behavior (Wagner, 2007) and ability to use nonverbal information (Wagner, 2008) should be considered relevant to the construct of listening comprehension. It follows that not only should video replace audio-only language learning materials in the classroom, but standardized tests of listening comprehension (e.g., the LC portion of the TOEFL) should include a video component for the sake of accurately measuring the LC construct. The exclusion of nonverbal information from audio-only listening tests may lead to unrealistically negative inferences about language learners' LC abilities in authentic communication scenarios.

Reading Comprehension

Literature examining the relationship between video viewing and reading comprehension in ESL classrooms is scarce. However, one recent study by Whiting and Granoff (2010) evaluated and compared the effects of audio and video input on college-level English language learners' short story reading comprehension. Participants were 37 English language learners enrolled in a college ESL course. The students were divided into three groups; each group was asked to read Shirley Jackson's short story "The Lottery" and discuss it among themselves. After the discussion, those in the audio group listened to an audiotaped reading of the text, and those in the video group watched videotaped dramatization of the story; those in the control group received no additional exposure to the story. Reading comprehension in all three groups was evaluated by seven open-ended questions that were presented immediately after discussion. The audio and video groups answered the same seven questions again following their second exposure to the story. Whiting and Granoff report greatly improved comprehension among those in the video group from pretest to posttest, whereas only some students in the audio group benefited from the treatment—most did not change their answers significantly and showed levels of comprehension similar to the control group. It is also worth noting that even low-achieving readers benefited from the video input.

To account for their results, Whiting and Granoff (2010) suggest that video input allowed learners to fully utilize their oral language competence while also providing contextual information that was helpful for recalling and thinking more deeply about the text. This study provides preliminary evidence that video input can serve as an effective supplement to traditional reading instruction. Interestingly, despite the difference in comprehension gains between the audio and video groups, participants in both groups reported that the additional input was appealing to them. Likewise, both forms of input provoked emotional reactions to the story, suggesting that both audio and video may be useful for increasing learners' engagement with text.

Vocabulary Acquisition

Smidt and Hegelheimer (2004) evaluated the effect of various types of video input on vocabulary acquisition in the ESL classroom. Participants were 24 college-level ESL learners who were divided into three groups (i.e., low-, mid-, and high-performance) based on their scores on a vocabulary dictation pretest. A 15-minute academic lecture on horticulture in video format was then presented to each participant on a computer. The lecture consisted of three types of segments: (1) a full-screen view of the lecturer as a talking head; (2) key words from the lecture presented as overhead transparencies, with the talking head in the corner of the screen; and (3) the full-screen display of picture-based slides illustrating key concepts. Both an immediate and a delayed posttest of the same lexical items were employed to evaluate vocabulary acquisition and retention. Results show that the mean performance on vocabulary measures improved significantly relative to the pretest. Moreover, the results of the immediate posttest were not significantly different from those of the delayed posttest, indicating that vocabulary gains were retained. Smidt and Hegelheimer suggest that the computer-based task enabled incidental vocabulary acquisition by giving students multimodal exposure to lexical items through aural presentation (via the lecture), written repetition (via the overhead transparencies), and pictorial depictions (via the slides).

Fluency and Accuracy in Language Production

Two studies of adult ESL learners in the United States provide preliminary evidence that the instructional use of video tasks can help improve the fluency and accuracy of language production, for the purposes of communicating via online chat and giving an oral presentation, respectively.

In the first study, Arslanyilmaz and Pedersen (2010) divided a class of intermediate-level ESL students (N = 20) into two groups and had each member of one group paired with a member of the other. The groups were split up into two computer labs, and pairs collaborated remotely via online chat in a digital learning environment to complete a variety of language-based tasks in "authentic" hypothetical scenarios (e.g., imagining they were roommates picking out Christmas gifts for all four members of a described American home-stay family). Five pairs were given access to captioned videos of native English speakers performing a similar task, and the remaining five pairs were given no such access. Over the course of four hour-long task sessions, the pairs who had access to captioned videos produced significantly more fluent and accurate language via the online chat tool, even when controlling for computer proficiency skills. However, because the videos featured tasks very similar to those on which the students were collaborating, it is unclear whether the observed effects would generalize to the performance of unrelated language tasks. Furthermore, questions remain as to whether the increased fluency and accuracy would extend to oral language, more formal written language, or both; as Arslanyilmaz and Pedersen point out, the distinct type of language used for online chat shares characteristics of both more traditional writing and spoken conversation. The fact that the authors found no significant difference between the video and no-video groups on measures of syntactic or lexical complexity, both common features of academic writing skill, suggests that the observed differences may be more directly linked to oral communicative abilities.

In support of this hypothesized link between the use of video-based tasks and improvements in oral production, Hardison (2005) found that Chinese graduate students in the United States with advanced levels of English proficiency who watched contextualized video clips as part of a one-on-one language training program improved their spoken prosody more than those who listened to audio clips as part of the same training. Participants ($N = 28$) were divided into four groups in a 2 x 2 design with mode of input (audio vs. video) and contextualization of speech clips (isolated sentences vs. meaningful paragraph-length utterances). The audio and video training materials were taken from participants' own 10-minute recorded presentations about topics of personal interest. Participants were asked to give similarly structured presentations about different topics after the training as well, and all video recordings of (pre- and posttraining) presentations were evaluated by native English speakers. All groups improved their prosody as a result of training, but there were significant differences in the four groups. The most improvement was observed in the group who saw contextualized (i.e., paragraph-length) video clips. Participants who listened to contextualized audio clips demonstrated similar levels of prosody improvement as those who watched video clips of isolated sentences. Not surprisingly, those who listened to sentence-level audio clips experienced the least improvement of all.

ASPECTS OF VIDEO THAT AFFECT LEARNING

Despite the growing evidence that videos can have a positive impact on various language learning outcomes, all videos do not function equally well as instructional tools. Two aspects of ESL videos that have received significant research attention are authenticity and the presence of English captions.

Authenticity of Video Content

The authenticity of teaching materials is a heatedly discussed issue in the domain of second language teaching. Gilmore (2007) points out that "authenticity" is an ambiguous concept, noting that it "can be situated in either the text itself, in the participants, in the social or cultural situation and purposes of the communicative act, or some combination of these" (p. 98). For the purposes of the present review, *authentic materials* are defined as materials in which (1) the language employed is naturalistic, rather than contrived instructional language that compresses key words into highly scripted dialogues, and (2) the content can be readily applied to the language learners' lives outside the classroom for purposes of communication. Although the gap between authentic language and textbook language has been well documented (Gilmore, 2007), the authenticity of newer video-based language has been somewhat less discussed.

South, Gabbitas, and Merrill (2008) recently compared video-based nonnarrative language models with narrative models, arguing that the latter were preferable for ESL teaching. All videos were embedded in instructional software being developed by the authors. The two narrative videos were each between 40 and 45 minutes long and were followed by listening comprehension, vocabulary, and grammar exercises. The decontextualized segments were 3 to 5 minutes long, each containing many of the same key words, phrases, and grammatical features as the narrative videos. A group of ESL students ($N = 20$) in a U.S. high school viewed all videos as part of a general pilot testing of the language learning software. Participants were then interviewed about their experience; they reported that the language in the narrative videos was both highly engaging and informative, whereas the shorter segments were rated as lacking both informational and emotional appeal. South et al. suggest that the narrative videos engaged language learners by presenting intriguing plots and characters in authentic linguistic and cultural contexts.

Hardison's (2005) study provides further evidence of the importance of authenticity and context. Because the training materials in this study were audio and video clips taken from participants' own unscripted presentations about topics of interest, they can generally be assumed to be authentic and relevant to the students. Furthermore, the fact that the sentence-level audio group performed significantly worse than all other groups suggests that contextualization of the speech used in the clips appeared to be just as important as mode of input (audio-only vs. audio + video). The paragraph-level audio group performed at a similar level as the sentence-level video group, suggesting video input may compensate for a lack of language context. In a follow-up questionnaire, participants who saw the paragraph-level video clips expressed the highest level of satisfaction with the training, indicating that authentic video material presented in context may have also had positive effects on learners' motivation.

English Captions in Video

Although the term *captions* (also called *subtitles*) can technically refer to any text that appears on screen during a video, it is more narrowly defined in the presently reviewed research as the exact script of spoken utterances presented simultaneously with the utterances themselves. Although captioning options for TV and video programs have existed for decades primarily for the benefit of the deaf and hard of hearing, the use of captions for second language learning is a relatively new phenomenon (Vanderplank, 2010). However, the past 15 years have seen the emergence of a substantial body of research documenting how the use of video with English captions affects the language learning outcomes of ESL students in the United States.

In a study conducted by Huang and Eskey (1999), adult ESL students ($N = 30$) with intermediate levels of English proficiency watched an episode of a made-for-ESL program called *Family Album U.S.A.* and then completed an aurally presented multiple-choice LC test based on the video clip. Although all participants watched the same clip, English captions were only available to a randomly selected half. The group that saw captions performed significantly better on the LC test, which was modeled on the LC portion of the TOEFL and included questions assessing both vocabulary acquisition and general comprehension of the content of the video clip. Demographic variables such as length of ESL exposure, age of starting ESL learning, and length of time in the United States were not correlated with scores on the LC measures employed in the study, further strengthening the interpretation that captions accounted for the difference between the two groups. On a questionnaire given after the LC test, participants in both groups reported that captions helped (captions group) or would have helped (no-captions group) their listening ability, comprehension, and vocabulary acquisition.

In a larger scale study, Markham (1999) examined the effects of captioning on listening word recognition among 118 adult ESL students. Participants were selected from a college intensive ESL program based on their advanced levels of English proficiency, as determined by TOEFL scores ranging from 550 to 570. All participants watched two video clips taken from authentic educational TV programs; one clip was about whales and had a high audio/video correlation (i.e., the video often corresponded to the audio narration), and the other dealt with civil rights in the United States and had a very low audio/video correlation (i.e., the video seldom matched what was being spoken by the narrator). These two clips were viewed either with or without captions, and the order in which the two clips were presented was alternated across groups of students. For example, one group saw the whale clip without captions followed by the civil rights clip with captions, another group saw the civil rights clip with captions followed by the whale clip with captions, and yet another group saw the whale clip with captions followed by the civil rights clip without captions. Following the presentation of each video clip, students were given a 50-item multiple-choice test of listening word recognition in which they had to identify which word (out of four possible options) appeared in an aurally presented sentence. All target words had appeared in the preceding video clip. Consistent with the findings of Huang and Eskey (1999), individual demographic variables (e.g., time spent in the United States, reported prior knowledge of the topic, academic major) were not significantly related to word recognition. However, students who had seen captions performed significantly better than those who had not. These results were consistent across both video types, indicating that audio/video correlation did not interact with the presence of captions. These results suggest that the benefits of captions on LC also extend to more basic aural word recognition.

Markham (2001) also found that the usefulness of captions to ESL learners depended on cultural background knowledge of the video topic. Using a design similar to that of his 1999 study, Markham showed informational video clips about Buddhist and Muslim rituals, either with or without captions, to a group of 79 ESL students with advanced levels of proficiency. Students identified themselves as Buddhist ($n = 9$), Muslim ($n = 16$), or religion neutral ($n = 54$). Among Muslim students, the presence or absence of captions had no effect on the number of ideas expressed in written summaries of the Muslim video, whereas those who saw captions with the Buddhist video produced significantly more elaborate summaries than those who saw no captions. For the religion neutral students, who reported little prior background knowledge about either religion, the presence of captions had a significant effect on the quality of written summaries of both videos; those who watched videos with captions produced significantly more ideas regardless of the video content. Although the results were somewhat less clear with Buddhist students, Markham attributes this to the particularly small sample size of that group. These results suggest that captions are most useful in videos on topics about which students had little cultural background knowledge—the very types of videos to which international ESL students are typically exposed in the United States

More recently, Grgurović and Hegelheimer (2007) examined the effects of text-based help options (i.e., captions and scripts) to scaffold listening comprehension in a digital learning environment. In their study, 18 adult ESL students watched a video lecture about astronomy as part of an Academic English Listening course. The lecture was presented to students individually via computers and was divided into ten 1-minute segments. After each segment, students were given one multiple-choice comprehension question; a correct answer prompted the next segment of the lecture, whereas an incorrect answer required students to watch the segment again. Prior to this second viewing, students were prompted to choose between help options; they could either watch the video with real-time captions or watch it with a transcript of the entire lecture displayed alongside. Participants used captions more frequently than transcripts, and they also kept the caption-based windows open significantly longer than the transcript-based windows. Surveys given both before and after the experiment indicated that the majority ($n = 13$) of students were more familiar with captions than transcripts and also preferred captions as a form of help. Interestingly, higher proficiency students tended to view captions for significantly more time than lower proficiency students, who mostly closed the help window immediately, exhibiting a pattern of noninteraction with help options. This finding suggests that higher proficiency levels may result in the more effective use of captions to repair comprehension breakdowns. Interaction with help options also predicted performance on comprehension posttests given immediately after the lecture and 1 week later, indicating that the use of captions and/or transcripts led to higher retention of the material covered in the lecture.

In sum, although captions are often viewed by teachers as hindering the development of listening skills due to an overreliance on written text (Danan, 2004), the results of studies designed specifically to isolate listening skills by assessing listening comprehension using exclusively oral language (e.g., Huang & Eskey, 1999; Markham, 1999) show that caption availability actually leads to better LC among adult ESL learners above and beyond improvements in reading and writing abilities. The authors of these studies suggest that these improvements are at least partially due to the positive effects of bimodal presentation (i.e., the use of both audio and visual input pathways) on language processing.

Smidt and Hegelheimer's (2004) study provides further support of the efficacy of bimodal presentation on listening comprehension. They found that adult ESL students performed better on LC test questions that were based on picture-based slides or text-based transparencies outlining a video lecture's main points, relative to test questions that were based on the audio/video lecture alone. Though these differences were not statistically significant, they suggest that pairing text, speech, and images may result in better comprehension.

IMPLICATIONS FOR PRACTITIONERS

The research literature reviewed here has several important implications for teachers of ESL students in the United States. Although research strongly supports the integration of digital video into language learning and teaching, it also suggests that teachers pay close attention to students' levels of English proficiency and background knowledge when making instructional decisions regarding video. For instance, King (2002) warns ESL instructors that learners with low proficiency levels may experience overload of their language processing capabilities when presented with authentic videos. Similarly, Vanderplank (2010) suggests that English captions may overwhelm low-proficiency learners with incomprehensible language information and suggests that captions in students' first language are more appropriate scaffolds for these learners. When teaching intermediate- and advanced-level students such as the participants in most of the studies reviewed in this chapter, the pedagogical value of using video appears to be significant, and English captions may be particularly useful when these learners lack background knowledge of the topic covered by the video (Markham, 2001).

ESL practitioners looking to incorporate video into classrooms or digital learning environments must also consider issues of content authenticity and appropriateness for language learning. Made-for-ESL narrative videos featuring authentic language such as *Family Album U.S.A.* are ideal instructional tools that gradually increase language difficulty to accommodate learners' growth (i.e., Huang & Eskey, 1999), but South et al. (2008) note that the design and production of such authentic narrative videos for the purposes of language learning could be quite costly, with high production quality relying on professional actors, script writers, and producers. In a modern society saturated with professionally produced narrative videos of all kinds, viewers are accustomed to such high production quality and may not be interested in lower quality videos. The production and promotion of made-for-ESL videos as teaching tools may therefore not be feasible for schools or smaller organizations with limited financial resources.

On the other hand, videos produced for other purposes (e.g., clips from feature films, television programs, or documentaries) can be, and often are, incorporated into classrooms along with teacher-created exercises that focus on particular language learning objectives. Such videos feature more contextual information and authentic language than purely instructional materials (e.g., those used by Wagner, 2010), providing a potential source for learners to gain insight on how English is used in various cultural situations outside the classroom. Many adult ESL learners in the United States may indeed be unfamiliar with aspects of U.S. culture and could thus benefit from the cultural content of carefully selected authentic videos.

Of course, even if the content of a given professionally produced narrative video is relevant to certain language tasks and is highly engaging, other features of the video, such as difficult accents, fast rates of speech, or a convoluted plotline, might hinder comprehension and even lead to frustration among language learners (King, 2002). In addition, Smidt and Hegelheimer (2004) suggest that poor readers were more easily distracted by the multitude of cues in an authentic video. Because authentic videos are generally longer and more complex than purely instructional video clips, we suggest that practitioners strike a pragmatic balance between video authenticity and the comprehension capacities of ESL students.

DIRECTIONS FOR FUTURE RESEARCH

Based on the present literature review, three directions are suggested for future research to shed further light on the role of video in language learning and teaching. First, all of the research reviewed in this chapter (with the exception of South et al., 2008) was done with adult participants, and most studies were specifically focused on international college or graduate students. Thus, the effects of video on the language learning outcomes of younger ESL students (i.e., children and adolescents) in the United States are still largely undocumented. These learners are in crucial stages of language development, and future research should examine whether the various findings of studies in the present review generalize to specific language learning outcomes in these populations.

A second limitation stems from the fact that many of the results reported in the present literature review were based on studies using small sample sizes, qualitative methodologies, or self-report measures. More large-scale, controlled experiments with quantitative measures are still needed to confirm these preliminary findings and further clarify the nature of the relationships between the use of digital video and various aspects of second language acquisition.

Finally, all of the current research examines students' learning outcomes over relatively short periods of time. Although Hardison's (2005) study involved several weeks of fairly intensive training and is thus a notable exception, most other studies dealt with one or more sessions within a timeframe of several days. The literature reviewed here thus offers little insight into the long-term effects of various types of video-assisted language learning on ESL students. In the interest of providing a more solid evidence base to inform the current trend of video use in ESL curricula (Vanderplank, 2010), longitudinal studies should be conducted in classroom settings with integrated video or CALL elements. Such studies could examine the development of English listening comprehension over periods of months or years using video-based tests such as the one developed by Wagner (2010). By also employing large sample sizes, longitudinal research could study the role of different kinds of video input (e.g., authentic narratives vs. short decontextualized clips, videos with captions in the first and second language vs. those without captions) in the long-term development of general language production and comprehension using standardized measures such as the TOEFL.

References

Ajayi, L. (2012). Video "reading" and multimodality: A study of ESL/literacy pupils' interpretation of *Cinderella* from their socio-historical perspective. *Urban Review, 44,* 60–89. doi:10.1007/s11256-011-0175-0

Albers, P., & Sanders, J. (Eds.). (2010). *Literacies, the arts, and multimodality.* Urbana, IL: National Council of Teachers of English.

Al-Seghayer, K. (2001). The effect of multimedia annotation modes on L2 vocabulary acquisition: A comparative study. *Language Learning & Technology, 5*(1), 202–232. Retrieved from http://llt.msu.edu/

Ambrose, D. (2002). Finding new messages in television commercials. *English Teaching Forum Online, 40*(2), 44–46. Retrieved from http://exchanges.state.gov /englishteaching/forum-journal.html

Anderson, H. (1997). *Conversation, language and possibilities: A postmodern approach to therapy.* New York, NY: Basic Books.

Arslanyilmaz, A., & Pedersen, S. (2010). Improving language production using subtitled similar task videos. *Language Teaching Research, 14,* 377–395. doi:10.1177/ 1362168810375363

Atwood, M. (1969). *The edible woman.* Toronto, Ontario, Canada: McClelland and Stewart.

Augé, M. (1995). *Non-places: Introduction to an anthropology of supermodernity.* London, England: Verso.

August, D. L., & Shanahan, T. (Eds.). (2006). *Developing literacy in a second language: Report of the National Literacy Panel.* Mahwah, NJ: Lawrence Erlbaum.

Barton, D., & Hamilton, M. (1998). *Local literacies: Reading and writing in one community.* London, England: Routledge.

Biemiller, A. (2008). *Words worth teaching.* Columbus, OH: SRA/McGraw-Hill.

Bo-Kristensen, M., & Meyer, B. (2008). Transformations of the language laboratory. In T. Hansson (Ed.), *Handbook of research on digital information technologies: Innovations, methods, and ethical issues* (pp. 27–36). Hershey, PA: IGI Global. Retrieved from http://www.irma-international.org/viewtitle/19833/

Bolter, J. D., & Grusin, R. (1999). *Remediation: Understanding new media.* Cambridge: MIT Press.

Boyle, A. (2011, September 20). Gamers solve molecular puzzle that baffled scientists [Web log post]. Retrieved from http://cosmiclog.msnbc.msn.com /_news/2011/09/18/7802623-gamers-solve-molecular-puzzle-that-baffled-scientists

Brant, S. (2005). *Can Bart, Monika, Malcolm and Jerry help English language learners develop their listening skills? The use of sitcoms in the classroom.* Paper presented at the 18th Annual EA Education Conference. Retrieved from http:// qa.englishaustralia.com.au/index.cgi?E=hcatfuncs&PT=sl&X=getdoc&Lev1 =pub_c06_07&Lev2=c05_brandt

Brass, J. J. (2008). Local knowledge and digital movie composing in an after-school literacy program. *Journal of Adolescent and Adult Literacy, 51,* 464–473. doi:10.1598/ JAAL.51.6.3 10.1598/JAAL.51.6.3

Bublé, M., Chang, A., & Foster-Gillies, A. (2005). *Michael Bublé—Home lyrics.* Retrieved from http://www.lyrics007.com/Michael%20Buble%20Lyrics/Home %20Lyrics.html

Canale, M. (1983). From communicative competence to communicative language pedagogy. In J. C. Richards & R. W. Schmitt (Eds.), *Language and communication* (pp. 2–27). London, England: Longman.

Canale, M., & Swain, M. (1980). Theoretical bases of communicative approaches to second language teaching and testing. *Applied Linguistics, 1,* 1–47. doi:10.1093/ applin/1.1.1

Carlo, M. S., August, D., & Snow, C. (2005). Sustained vocabulary-learning strategy instruction for English-language learners. In E. H. Hiebert & M. L. Kamil (Eds.), *Teaching and learning vocabulary: Bringing research to practice* (pp. 137–154). Mahwah, NJ: Lawrence Erlbaum.

Carrington, V. (2005). Txting: The end of civilization (again)? *Cambridge Journal of Education, 35*(2), 161–175. doi:10.1080/03057640500146799

Carrington, V., & Marsh, J. (2005). Digital childhood and youth: New texts, new literacies. *Discourse: Studies in the Cultural Politics of Education, 26,* 279–285. doi:10.1080/01596300500199890

Cazden, C. B. (1997). Performance before competence: Assistance to child discourse in the zone of proximal development. In M. Cole, Y. Engestrom, & O. Vasquez (Eds.), *Mind, culture and activity: Seminal papers from the laboratory of comparative human cognition* (pp. 303–310). Cambridge, England: Cambridge University Press. Retrieved from http://books.google.com/books?id=Z4 WqwWken_kC&pg=PA303&lpg#v=onepage&q&f=false

Chamot, A. U., & O'Malley, J. M. (1987). The cognitive academic language learning approach: A bridge to the mainstream. *TESOL Quarterly, 21,* 227–249. doi:10.2307/3586733

Chen, H.-J. H. (2011). Developing and evaluating SynctoLearn, a fully automatic video and transcript synchronization tool for EFL learners. *Computer Assisted Language Learning, 24*, 117–130. doi:10.1080/09588221.2010.526947

Chomsky, N. (1965). *Aspects of the theory of syntax.* Cambridge, MA: MIT Press.

Chung, J.-M. (1999). The effects of using video texts supported with advance organizers and captions on Chinese college students' listening comprehension: An empirical study. *Foreign Language Annals, 32*, 295–307. doi:10.1111/j.1944-9720.1999.tb01342.x

Chung, J.-M. (2002). The effects of using two advance organizers with video texts for the teaching of listening in English. *Foreign Language Annals, 35*, 231–241. doi:10.1111/j.1944-9720.2002.tb03157.x

Citizenship and Immigration Canada. (2009). *Annual report to Parliament on immigration, 2008.* Retrieved from http://www.cic.gc.ca/EnGLIsh/resources/publications/annual-report2008/section1.asp

Cobb, T. (2006). *VocabProfile home.* Retrieved from http://www.lextutor.ca/vp/

Coiro, J., Knobel, M., Lankshear, C., & Leu, D. J. (Eds.). (2008). *Handbook of research on new literacies.* New York, NY: Lawrence Erlbaum.

Concerned Children's Advertisers. (n.d.). *The media literacy lesson plans and activities.* Available from http://play.longlivekids.ca/educator/media-literacy-lesson-plans-and-activities

Cope, B., & Kalantzis, M. (Eds.). (2000). *Multiliteracies: Literacy learning and the design of social futures.* London, England: Routledge/Falmer.

Cope, B., & Kalantzis, M. (2009). "Multiliteracies": New literacies, new learning. *Pedagogies, 4*, 164–195. doi:10.1080/15544800903076044

Cope, B., Kalantzis, M., & Lankshear, C. (2005). A contemporary project: An interview. *E-Learning and Digital Media, 2*, 192–207. doi:10.2304/elea.2005.2.2.6

Corder, S. P. (1966). Modem foreign language teaching by television. In A. Valdman (Ed.), *Trends in language teaching* (pp. 235–249). New York, NY: McGraw-Hill.

Cortés-Conde, F., & Boxer, D. (2002). Bilingual word-play in literary discourse: The creation of relational identity. *Language and Literature, 11*, 137–151. doi:10.1177/096394700201100203

Coxhead, A. (2000). A new academic word list. *TESOL Quarterly, 34*, 213–238. doi:10.2307/3587951

Coxhead, A., & Nation, P. (2001). The specialised vocabulary of English for academic purposes. In J. Flowerdew, & M. Peacock (Eds.), *Research perspectives on English for academic purposes* (pp. 252–267). Cambridge, England: Cambridge University Press.

Cuban, L. (2001). *Oversold and underused: Computers in the classroom*. Cambridge, MA: Harvard University Press.

Cummins, J. (1983). Conceptual and linguistic foundations of language assessment. In S. S. Seidner (Ed.), *Issues of language assessment: Language assessment and curriculum planning* (pp. 131–178). Wheaton, MD: National Clearinghouse for Bilingual Education.

Cummins, J. (1984). Wanted: A theoretical framework for relating language proficiency to academic achievement among bilingual students. In C. Rivera (Ed.), *Language proficiency and academic achievement* (pp. 2–19). Clevedon, England: Multilingual Matters.

Cummins, J. (2004). Using IT to create a zone of proximal development for academic language learning: A critical perspective on trends and possibilities. In C. Davison (Ed.), *Information technology and innovation in language education* (pp. 105–126). Hong Kong: Hong Kong University Press.

Cummins, J. (2009). Literacy and English-language learners: A shifting landscape for students, teachers, researchers, and policy makers. *Educational Researcher, 38*, 382–385. doi:10.3102/0013189X038005382

Cummins, J. (2011). *Putting the evidence back into evidence-based policies for underachieving students*. Strasbourg: Council of Europe Language Policy Division. Available at http://www.coe.int/t/dg4/linguistic/default_en.asp

Cummins, J., Bismilla, V., Chow, P., Cohen, S., Giampapa, F., Leoni, L., Sandhu, P., Sastri, P. (2005). Affirming identity in multilingual classrooms. *Educational Leadership, 63*(1), 38–43.

Cummins, J., Brown, K., & Sayers, D. (2007). *Literacy, technology, and diversity: Teaching for success in changing times*. Boston, MA: Pearson.

Cummins, J., & Early, M. (2011). *Identity texts: The collaborative creation of power in multilingual schools*. Stoke-on-Trent, England: Trentham Books.

Dagenais, D. (2008). Pratiques langagieres des enfants de familles immigrants a la maison et a l'école [Language practices of children from immigrant families at home and school]. *Revue des Sciences de l'Éducation, 34*, 351–376.

Dagenais, D., Armand, F., Maraillet, E. & Walsh, N. (2008). Collaboration and co-construction of knowledge during language awareness activities in a Canadian elementary school. *Language Awareness, 17*, 139–155. doi:10.1080/09658410802146685

Danan, M. (2004). Captioning and subtitling: Undervalued language learning strategies. *Meta, 49*(1), 67–77. doi:10.7202/009021ar

Daniels, P. (2004). Video Bytes II. *The Language Teacher, 28*(1), 56–57. Retrieved from http://jalt-publications.org/tlt

Davidson, C. (2011). *Now you see it: How the brain science of attention will transform the way we live, work, and learn.* New York, NY: Penguin.

Dhonau, S., & McAlpine, D. (2002). "Streaming" best practices: Using digital video-teaching segments in the FL/ESL methods course. *Foreign Language Annals, 35,* 632–636. doi:10.1111/j.1944-9720.2002.tb01901.x

Dunkel, A., Brill, S., & Kohl, B. (2002). The impact of self-instructional technology on language learning: A view of NASILP. In C. A. Spreen (Ed.), *New technologies and language learning: Cases in the less commonly taught languages* (pp. 97–120). Honolulu: University of Hawaii, Second Language Teaching & Curriculum Center.

Early, M., & Marshall, S. (2008). Adolescent ESL students' interpretation and appreciation of literary texts: A case study of multimodality. *Canadian Modern Language Review, 64,* 377–397. doi:10.1353/cml.2008.0041

Edwards, R., Ivanič, R., & Mannion, G. (2009). The scrumpled geographies of literacies for learning. *Discourse: Studies in the Cultural Politics of Education, 30,* 483–499. doi:10.1080/01596300903237248

Eisenstein, M., Shuller, S., & Bodman, J. (1987). Learning English with an invisible teacher: An experimental video approach. *System, 15,* 209–216. doi:10.1016/0346-251X(87)90069-8

Elleström, L. (2010). The modalities of media: A model of understanding intermedial relations. In L. Elleström (Ed.), *Media borders, multimodality and intermediality* (pp. 11–48). Basingstoke, England: Palgrave Macmillan.

Erkaya, O. (2005). TV commercials as authentic materials to teach communication, culture and critical thinking. *MEXTESOL, 29*(1), 2–18.

Foss, P., Carney, N., McDonald, K., & Rooks, M. (2007). Project-based learning activities for short-term intensive English programs. *Asian EFL Journal, 23.*

Frideres, J. S. (2006). Cities and immigrant integration: The future of second- and third-tier centres. *Our Diverse Cities, 2,* 3–8. Retrieved from http://www.metropolis.net/pdfs/ODC_2_Frideres_e.pdf

Fritsch, C. (1998). Student-led lesson: Vacation commercials. *Internet TESL Journal, 4*(9). Retrieved from http://iteslj.org

Fujita, E. (2012). *Emi Fujita, At the end of the day (le couple version) lyrics.* Retrieved from http://www.justsomelyrics.com/2472429/Emi-Fujita-At-The-End-Of-The-Day-(Le-Couple-Version)-Lyrics

Furman, F. (2005). The long road home: Migratory experience and the construction of the self. *Journal of Prevention and Intervention in the Community, 30,* 91–116. doi:10.1300/J005v30n01_08

Gai, B. (2009). A world through the camera phone lens: A case study of Beijing camera phone use. *Knowledge, Technology, and Policy, 22,* 195–204. doi:10.1007/ s12130-009-9084-x

Gairns, R., & Redman, S. (1986). *Working with words: A guide to teaching and learning vocabulary.* Cambridge, England: Cambridge University Press

García, O. (2009). *Bilingual education in the 21st century: A global perspective.* Chichester, England: Wiley-Blackwell.

Gardner, D. (1994). Creating simple interactive video for self-access. In D. Gardner & L. Miller (Eds.), *Directions in self-access language learning* (pp. 107–114). Hong Kong: Hong Kong University Press. Available from http://muse.jhu.edu/books /9789882200999?auth=0

Gee, J. P. (2003). *What video games have to teach us about learning and literacy?* New York, NY: Palgrave/Macmillan.

Gee, J. P. (2004). *Situated language and learning: A critique of traditional schooling.* New York, NY: Routledge.

Gee, J. P. (2008). Video games and embodiment. *Games and Culture, 3,* 253–263. doi:10.1177/1555412008317309

Gee, J. P., Hull, G., & Lankshear, C. (1996). *The new work order: Behind the language of the new capitalism.* Boulder, CO: Westview.

Giampapa, F. (2001). Hyphenated identities: Italian-Canadian youth and the negotiation of ethnic identities in Toronto. *International Journal of Bilingualism, 5,* 279–315. doi:10.1177/13670069010050030301

Gilmore, A. (2007). Authentic materials and authenticity in foreign language learning. *Language Teaching, 40*(2), 97–118. doi:10.1017/S0261444807004144

Glass, E. (1992). Notes from an olde-tyme producer of language videotapes. In S. Stempleski & P. Arcario (Eds.), *Video in second language teaching: Using, selecting and producing video for the classroom* (pp. 143–155). Alexandria, VA: TESOL.

Goldman, M. (1996). If you can read this, thank TV. *TESOL Journal, 6*(2), 15–18. doi:10.1016/S0889-4906(00)00003-X

Grayson, J. P. (2004). *ESL, ethno-racial origin and academic achievement of university students.* Unpublished manuscript, Atkinson Faculty of Liberal and Professional Studies, York University, Toronto, Ontario, Canada.

Grayson, J. P. (2008). The experiences and outcomes of domestic and international students at four Canadian universities. *Higher Education Research & Development, 27,* 215–230. doi:10.1080/07294360802183788

Grayson, J. P. (2009). Language background, ethno-racial origin, and academic achievement of students at a Canadian university. *International Migration, 47*(2), 33–67. doi:10.1111/j.1468-2435.2008.00481.x

Grgurović, M., & Hegelheimer, V. (2007). Help options and multimedia listening: Students' use of subtitles and the transcript. *Language Learning & Technology, 11*(1), 45–66. Retrieved from http://llt.msu.edu

Gromik, N. (2008). *Windows Movie Maker in the English as a foreign language class.* Retrieved from http://www.microsoft.com/education/highered/whitepapers/moviemaker/MovieMaker.aspx

Gromik, N. (2009a). Meaningful tasks with video in the ESOL classroom. In E. Hanson-Smith & S. Rilling (Eds.), *Learning Languages Through Technology* (pp. 109–123). Alexandria, VA: TESOL.

Gromik, N. (2009b). Producing cell phone video diaries. In M. Thomas (Ed.), *Handbook of research on web 2.0 and language learning.* Hershey, PA: Information Science Reference.

Gross, M. M. (1998). Analysis of human movement using digital video. *Journal of Educational Multimedia and Hypermedia, 7*(4), 375–395.

Guthrie, J. T. (2004). Teaching for literacy engagement. *Journal of Literacy Research, 36*(1), 1–30.

Haddix, M. P. (1999). *Just Ella.* New York, NY: Simon & Schuster Books for Young Readers.

Hague, C., & Williamson, B. (2009). *Digital participation, digital literacy, and school subjects: A review of the policies, literature and evidence.* Slough, England: Futurelab. Retrieved from http://www.futurelab.org.uk/sites/default/files/Digital_Participation_review.pdf

Handscombe, R. (1975). The Sunrunners: ESL by TV for grade 3 in Ontario. *TESOL Quarterly, 9,* 289–298. doi:10.2307/3585960

Hanley, J. E. B., Herron, C., & Cole, S. P. (1995). Using video as an advance organizer to a written passage in the FLES classroom. *Modern Language Journal, 79,* 57–66. doi:10.2307/329393

Hanson-Smith, E. (1997). *Technology in the classroom: Practice and promise in the 21st century* (TESOL Professional Papers #4). Alexandria, VA: TESOL.

Hanson-Smith, E. (2004). Video online: What's new? *Essential Teacher, 1*(5), 32–44.

Hanson-Smith, E. (2007). Classroom practice: Tasks for collaborative learning. In J. Egbert & E. Hanson-Smith (Eds.), *CALL environments: Research practice and critical issues* (2nd ed., pp. 194–208). Alexandria, VA: TESOL.

Hardison, D. M. (2005). Contextualized computer-based L2 prosody training: Evaluating the effects of discourse context and video input. *CALICO Journal, 22*(2), 175–190. Retrieved from https://calico.org/journalTOC.php?current=1

Harris, B. S. (2006). Video in education: A practical guide for teachers. *Meridian, 9*(1). Retrieved from http://www.ncsu.edu/meridian/index.html

Hatzigeourgiou, K. (2009). *Recognizing common advertising strategies.* Retrieved from http://schools.tdsb.on.ca/westhill/business/BBI/BBI-Unit-4/ADstrategies.pdf

Heath, S. B. (1983). *Ways with words: Language, life and work in communities and classrooms.* Cambridge, England: Cambridge University Press.

Heath, S. B., & McLaughlin, M. W. (Eds.). (1993). *Identity and inner-city youth.* New York, NY: Teachers College Press.

Henderson, M., Auld, G., Holkner, B., Russell, G., Seah, W. T., & Fernando, A. (2010). Students creating digital video in the primary classroom: Student autonomy, learning outcomes, and professional learning communities. *Australian Educational Computing, 24*(2), 12–20. Retrieved from http://acce.edu.au/journal

Herron, C., Cole, S. P., Corrie, C., & Dubreil, S. (1999). The effectiveness of a video-based curriculum in teaching culture. *Modern Language Journal, 83,* 518–533. doi:10.1111/0026-7902.00038 http://www.cic.gc.ca/EnGLIsh/resources /publications/annual-report2008/section1.asp

Huang, H.-C., & Eskey, D. E. (1999). The effects of closed-captioned television on the listening comprehension of intermediate English as a second language (ESL) students. *Journal of Educational Technology Systems, 28*(1), 75–96. doi:10.2190/ RG06-LYWB-216Y-R27G

Hughes, J. (2008). The "screen-size" art: Using digital media to perform poetry. *English in Education, 42,* 148–164. doi:10.1111/j.1754-8845.2008.00012.x

Hull, G. A. (2003). Youth culture and digital media: New literacies for new times. *Research in the Teaching of English, 38*(2), 229–233. Retrieved from http://www.jstor .org/action/showPublication?journalCode=resintheteacheng

Hull, G. A., & Katz, M. (2006). Creating an agentive self: Case studies of digital storytelling. *Research in the Teaching of English, 41*(1), 43–81.

Hull, G., & Nelson, M. E. (2005). Locating the semiotic power of multimodality. *Written Communication, 22,* 224–261. doi:10.1177/0741088304274170

Hull, G., & Stornaiuolo, A. (2010). Literate arts in a global world: Reframing social networking as cosmopolitan practice. *Journal of Adolescent and Adult Literacy, 54*(2), 85–97. doi:10.1598/JAAL.54.2.1

Hurston, Z. N. (1998). *Their eyes were watching God.* New York, NY: Perennial Classics. (Original work published 1937)

Hymes, D. (1972). On communicative competence. In J. B. Pride & J. Holmes (Eds.), *Sociolinguistics* (pp. 53–73). Harmondsworth, England: Penguin Books.

InfoTrends. (2007). *InfoTrends study shows increased use of camera phones among GenZers.* Retrieved from http://www.capv.com/public/Content/Press/2007 /10.23.07.html

InfoTrends. (2008). *Emerging markets driving growth in worldwide camera phone market.* Retrieved from http://www.infotrends.com/public/Content/Press/2008/07.29.2008.html

Institute of International Education. (2012). *International students in Canada.* Retrieved from http://www.iie.org/en/Services/Project-Atlas/Canada/International-Students-In-Canada

International Society for Technology in Education. (2012). *ISTE NETS-S: Advancing digital age learning.* Retrieved from http://www.iste.org/standards/nets-for-students.aspx

Jenkins, H. (2008). Media literacy: Who needs it? In T. Willoughby & E. Wood (Eds.), *Children's learning in a digital world* (pp. 15–39). Malden, MA: Blackwell. doi:10.1002/9780470696682.ch1

Juhasz, A. (2011). *Learning from YouTube: Glossary.* Cambridge, MA: MIT Press. Retrieved from http://vectors.usc.edu/projects/learningfromyoutube/glossary.php#42

Katchen, J., Morris, B., & Savova, L. (2005). Do-it-yourself video role models. *Essential Teacher, 2*(1), 40–43.

Kearney, M., & Schuck, S. (2004). *Students in the director's seat: Teaching and learning across the school curriculum with student-generated video.* Retrieved from http://engage.wisc.edu/dma/research/docs/Kearney-StudentsDirectorsSeat.pdf

Kellner, D. (2004). Technological transformation, multiple literacies and the re-visioning of education. *E-Learning and Digital Media, 1*(1), 9–37. doi:10.2304/elea.2004.1.1.8

Kennedy, C., & Levy, M. (2008). L'italiano al telefonino: Using SMS to support beginners' language learning. *ReCALL, 20,* 315–330. doi:10.1017/S0958344008000530

King, J. (2002). Using DVD feature films in the EFL classroom. *Computer Assisted Language Learning, 15,* 509–523. doi:10.1076/call.15.5.509.13468

King, K., & Ganuza, N. (2005). Language, identity, education, and transmigration: Chilean adolescents in Sweden. *Journal of Language, Identity and Education, 4*(3), 179–199. doi:10.1207/s15327701jlie0403_1

Knobel, M., & Lankshear, C. (2008). Remix: The art and craft of endless hybridization. *Journal of Adolescent and Adult Literacy, 52,* 22–33. doi:10.1598/JAAL.52.1.3

Kouritzin, S. (2006). Songs from taboo tongues: Experiencing first language loss. *Language and Literacy, 8*(1), 1–28. Retrieved from https://ejournals.library.ualberta.ca/index.php/langandlit/index

Kress, G. (2000). Multimodality: Challenges to thinking about language. *TESOL Quarterly, 34,* 337–340. doi:10.2307/3587959

Kress, G. (2003). *Literacy in the new media age.* London, England: Routledge.

Kress, G., & Van Leeuwen, T. (1996). *Reading images: The grammar of visual design.* London, England: Routledge.

Lam, S., Cheng, R. W., & Choy, H. C. (2010). School support and teacher motivation to implement project-based learning. *Learning and Instruction, 20,* 487–497. doi:10.1016/j.learninstruc.2009.07.003

Lankshear, C., & Knobel, M. (2006). *New literacies: Everyday practices and classroom learning* (2nd ed.). Maidenhead, England: Open University Press and McGraw-Hill Education.

Lantolf, J. (2006). Sociocultural theory and L2: State of the art. *Studies in Second Language Acquisition, 28,* 67–109. doi:10.1017/S0272263106060037

Lantolf, J. (2007). Conceptual knowledge and instructed second language learning: A sociocultural perspective. In S. Fotos & H. Nassaji (Eds.), *Form focused instruction and teacher education: Studies in honour of Rod Ellis* (pp. 35–54). Oxford, England: Oxford University Press.

Lantolf, J., & Thorne, S. (2006). *Sociocultural theory and the genesis of L2 development.* Oxford, England: Oxford University Press.

Laufer, B., & Nation, P. (1999). A vocabulary size test of controlled productive ability. *Language Testing, 16,* 33–51. doi:10.1177/026553229901600103

Lems, K. (2005). Music works: Music for adult English language learners. *New Directions for Adult and Continuing Education, 107,* 13–21. doi:10.1002/ace.185

Leung, C. (2005). Convivial communication: Recontextualizing communicative competence. *International Journal of Applied Linguistics, 15,* 119–144. doi:10.1111/j.1473-4192.2005.00084.x

Levy, M., & Kennedy, C. (2004). A task-cycling pedagogy using stimulated reflection and audio-conferencing in foreign language learning. *Language Learning & Technology, 8*(2), 50–68. Retrieved from http://llt.msu.edu/

Li, J., & McComb, B. (2011). Enhancing ESL students' vocabulary acquisition through a meaningful filmmaking project. *EUROCALL Review, 18,* 66–74. Retrieved from http://www.eurocall-languages.org/review/index.html

Li, J., & Snow, C. (2012). Orientations toward using social media, digital and mobile technologies to improve literacy skills among diverse students in urban schools. In S. Van Nuland & J. C. Greenlaw (Eds.), *Proceeding of the Conference on Teacher Education, Social Media and Teacher Learning* (pp. 61–70). Ottawa, Ontario, Canada: UOIT E-Press. Retrieved from http://shared.uoit.ca/shared/faculty/fed/documents/Social_Media_and_Teacher_Learning.pdf#page=67

Liao, J. (2000). *A chance of sunshine (turn left, turn right).* Mankato, MN: Creative Editions.

Liao, J. (2006). *Never ending story.* Taipei, Taiwan: Jimmy S.P.A.

Liao, J. (2009). *The fish with a smile.* New York, NY: Little, Brown.

Liao, J., & Thompson, S. (2006). *The sound of colors.* New York, NY: Little, Brown.

Lidwell, W., Holden, K., & Butler, J. (2003). *Universal principles of design.* Beverly, MA: Rockport.

Littlewood, W. (2003). Task-based language teaching: Theory and practice. *ACELT Journal, 7*(1), 3–13.

Lively, T., Snow, C., & August, D. (2003). *Vocabulary improvement program for English language: Learners and their classmates.* Baltimore, MD: Paul H. Brookes.

Lotherington, H. (2004). What four skills? Redefining language and literacy standards for ELT in the digital era. *TESL Canada Journal, 22*(1), 64–78.

Lotherington, H. (2011). *Pedagogy of multiliteracies: Rewriting Goldilocks.* New York, NY: Routledge.

Lotherington, H., & Sinitskaya Ronda, N. (2012). Multimodal literacies and assessment: Uncharted challenges in the English classroom. In C. Leung & B. Street (Eds.), *English—A changing medium for education* (pp. 104–128). Clevedon, England: Multilingual Matters.

Louw, K. J., Derwing, T., & Abbott, M. L. (2010). Teaching pragmatics to L2 learners for the workplace: The job interview. *Canadian Modern Language Review, 66,* 739–758. doi:10.3138/cmlr.66.5.739

Lu, M. (2008). Effectiveness of vocabulary learning via mobile phone. *Journal of Computer Assisted Learning, 24,* 515–525. doi:10.1111/j.1365-2729.2008.00289.x

Lyon, G. E. (n.d.). *Where I'm from.* Retrieved from http://www.georgeellalyon.com/where.html

Making picture books for adults. (2003, January 10). *Taipei Times.* Retrieved from http://www.taipeitimes.com/News/taiwan/archives/2003/01/10/190417

Manyak, P. C. (2004). "What did she say?" Translation in a primary-grade English immersion class. *Multicultural Perspectives, 6,* 12–18.

Markham, P. (1999). Captioned videotapes and second-language listening word recognition. *Foreign Language Annals, 32,* 321–328. doi:10.1111/j.1944-9720.1999.tb01344.x

Markham, P. (2001). The influence of culture-specific background knowledge and captions on second language comprehension. *Journal of Educational Technology Systems, 29,* 331–343. doi:10.2190/15TA-GX8P-74XP-YUA1

Markham, P., Peter, L., & McCarthey, T. (2001). The effects of native language vs. target language captions on foreign language students' DVD video comprehension. *Foreign Language Annals, 34,* 439–445. doi:10.1111/j.1944-9720.2001.tb02083.x

Marsh, J. (2006). Global, local/public, private: Young children's engagement in digital literacy practices in the home. In K. Pahl & J. Rowsell (Eds.), *Travel notes from the New Literacy Studies: Instances of practice* (pp. 19–38). Clevedon, England: Multilingual Matters.

McGee, K., & Fujita, T. (2001). Analyzing and creating TV commercials. In K. Ford & E. McCafferty (Eds.), *Projects from the university classroom* (pp. 115–136). Tokyo: Japan Association for Language Teaching, College and University Educators Special Interest Group.

McLean, D. (1971). *Vincent (Starry Starry Night)*. Retrieved from http://www.don -mclean.com/vincent.asp

McLuhan, M. (1962). *The Gutenberg galaxy: The making of typographic man*. Toronto, Ontario, Canada: University of Toronto Press.

McLuhan, M. (1964). *Understanding media: The extensions of man*. New York, NY: McGraw-Hill.

Measor, L., & Sikes, P. (1992). Visiting lives: Ethics and methodology in life history. In Ivor Goodson (Ed.), *Studying teachers' lives* (pp. 209–233). New York, NY: Teachers College Press.

Media Education Foundation. (2005). *Deconstructing an advertisement*. Retrieved from http://www.mediaed.org/Handouts/DeconstructinganAd.pdf

Microsoft. (2012). *Movie Maker*. Retrieved from http://windows.microsoft.com /en-US/windows-live/movie-maker-get-started

Miles, M. (1994). *Qualitative data analysis: An expanded handbook*. Thousand Oaks, CA: Sage.

Miller, P. (1994). Narrative practices: Their role in socialization and self-construction. In U. Neisser & R. Fivush (Eds.), *The remembering self: Construction and agency in self narrative* (pp. 158–179). Cambridge, England: Cambridge University Press.

Mills, K. A. (2010a). "Filming in progress": New spaces for multimodal designing. *Linguistics and Education, 21*, 14–28. doi:10.1016/j.linged.2009.12.003

Mills, K. A. (2010b). A review of the "digital turn" in the New Literacy Studies. *Review of Educational Research, 80*, 246–271. doi:10.3102/0034654310364401

Moore, E. (2011). *71% of online adults now use video-sharing sites*. Retrieved from http://pewinternet.org/~/media//Files/Reports/2011/Video%20sharing %202011.pdf

Morgan, B. (1997). Identity and intonation: Linking dynamic processes in an ESL classroom. *TESOL Quarterly, 31*, 431–450. doi:10.2307/3587833

Mossberger, K., Tolbert, J. C., & Stansbury, M. (2003). *Virtual inequality: Beyond the digital divide*. Washington, DC: Georgetown University Press.

Nagy, W. E., & Anderson, R. C. (1984). How many words are there in printed school English? *Reading Research Quarterly, 19*, 304–330. doi:10.2307/747823

Nahachewsky, J., & Begoray, D. (2010). Authoring the textual classroom in digital times. *Changing English: Studies in Culture and Education, 17*, 421–431. doi:10.1080/1358684X.2010.528877

Nakazaki, C. (2011). *Advertising techniques: 8th grade language arts.* Retrieved from http://www.slideshare.net/cnakazaki/advertising-techniques-7669052

Nation, P. (2001). *Learning vocabulary in another language.* Cambridge, England: Cambridge University Press.

National Council of Teachers of English. (2008). *The NCTE definition of 21st century literacies.* Retrieved from http://www.ncte.org/positions/statements/21stcentdefinition

National Standards in Foreign Language Education Project. (1999). *Standards for foreign language learning in the 21st century.* Lawrence, KS: Allen Press.

New London Group. (1996). A pedagogy of multiliteracies: Designing social futures. *Harvard Educational Review, 66*(1), 60–92.

Nikitina, L. (2011). Creating an authentic learning environment in the foreign language classroom. *International Journal of Instruction, 4*(1), 33–46.

Norquay, N. (1999). Identity and forgetting. *Oral History Review, 26*(1), 1–21. doi:10.1093/ohr/26.1.1

Norton Peirce, B. (1995). Social identity, investment, and language learning. *TESOL Quarterly, 29*, 9–31. doi:10.2307/3587803

Okabe, D., & Ito, M. (2003). Camera phones changing the definition of picture-worthy. *Japan Media Review.* Retrieved from http://www.ojr.org/japan/

Ong, W. J. (1980). Literacy and orality in our times. *Journal of Communication, 30*(1), 197–204. doi:10.1111/j.1460-2466.1980.tb01787.x

Ong, W. J. (1982). *Orality and literacy: The technologizing of the word.* London, England: Routledge.

Ontario Ministry of Education. (2005). *Many roots many voices: Supporting English language learners in every classroom.* Toronto, Ontario, Canada: Queens Printer for Ontario.

Ontario Ministry of Education. (2006). *Language: The Ontario curriculum grades 1–8.* Toronto, Ontario, Canada: Queens Printer for Ontario.

Ontario Ministry of Education. (2008). *Supporting English language learners: A practical guide for Ontario educators grades 1–8.* Toronto, Ontario, Canada: Queens Printer for Ontario.

Pahl, K., & Rowsell, J. (Eds.). (2006). *Travel notes from the New Literacy Studies: Instances of practice.* Clevedon, England: Multilingual Matters.

Pearlman, B. (2006). *Students thrive on cooperation and problem solving.* Retrieved from http://www.edutopia.org/new-skills-new-century?page=1

Portes, A., & Rumbaut, R. G. (2001). *Legacies: The story of the immigrant second generation.* Berkeley: University of California Press.

Purcell, K. (2010). *Teens, the Internet, and communication technology: A Pew Internet guide to online teens.* Retrieved from http://www.pewinternet.org/~/media/Files/Presentations/2010/Jun/Purcell%20YALSA%20pdf.pdf

Purcell-Gates, V., Jacobson, E., & Degener, S. (2004). *Print literacy development: Uniting cognitive and social practice theories.* Cambridge, MA: Harvard University Press.

Qadeer, M. A. (2003). *Ethnic segregation in a multicultural city: The case of Toronto, Canada* (CERIS Working Paper No. 28). Toronto, Ontario, Canada: CERIS. Retrieved from http://www.ceris.metropolis.net/wp-content/uploads/pdf/research_publication/working_papers/wp28.pdf

Qatar University, Office of Institutional Research and Data Warehouse. (n.d.). *Fast facts 2010–11 annual.* Qatar University. Retrieved from http://www.qu.edu.qa/offices/oipd/institutional_research/documents/Brochure/Fast_Facts_2010-11.pdf

Reimann, A. (2002). Music as a medium for language & cultural content instruction. *Canadian Content, 12*(3), 1–6.

Reitz, J. G., & Banerjee, R. (2007). Racial inequality, social cohesion and policy issues in Canada. In K. Banting, T. Courchene, & F. Seidle (Eds.), *Belonging? Diversity recognition and shared citizenship in Canada* (pp. 489–545). Montreal, Quebec, Canada: Institute for Research on Public Policy. Retrieved from http://www.irpp.org/books/archive/aots3/reitz.pdf

Rhodes, J. A., & Robnolt, V. J. (2009). Digital literacies in the classroom. In L. Christenbury, R. Bomer, & P. Smagorinsky (Eds.), *Handbook of adolescent literacy research* (pp. 153–169). New York, NY: Guilford Press.

Ribé, R., & Vidal, N. (1993). *Project work: Step by step.* Oxford, England: Heinemann.

Rideout, J. V., Foehr, G. U., & Roberts, F. D. (2010). *Generation M²: Media in the lives of 8- to 18-year-olds.* Menlo Park, CA: Henry J. Kaiser Family Foundation. Retrieved from http://www.kff.org/entmedia/upload/8010.pdf

Rogoff, B. (2003). *The cultural nature of human development.* Oxford, England: Oxford University Press.

Rosales, R. (2006). *The elements of online journalism.* Lincoln, NE: iUniverse Books.

Rose, D., & Dalton, B. (2009). Learning to read in the digital age. *Mind, Brain, and Education, 3*(2), 74–83. doi:10.1111/j.1751-228X.2009.01057.x

Rosenblatt, L. M. (1995). *Literature as exploration.* New York, NY: Modern Language Association.

Rowland, J. L. (2007). Closed-captioned video and the ESL classroom: A multi-sensory approach. *Journal of Adult Education, 36*(2), 35–39.

Rubin, A., Bresnahan, S., & Ducas, T. (1996). Cartwheeling through CamMotion. *Communications of the ACM, 39*(8), 84–85. doi:10.1145/232014.232035

San Diego County Board of Education. (2012). *Production tips in innovative video.* Retrieved from http://www.ivieawards.org/tips/

San Diego County Office of Education. (2009). *6th grade language arts—Propaganda.* Retrieved from http://picturethis.sdcoe.net/resources/Integrate_This/sell_it.pdf

Sanford, K., & Madill, L. (2008). Teachers and students learning through videogame design. In R. Ferdig (Ed.), *Handbook of research on effective electronic gaming in education* (pp. 345–357). Hershey, PA: Information Science Reference.

Savignon, S. J. (1972). *Communicative competence: An experiment in foreign language teaching.* Philadelphia, PA: Center for Curriculum Development.

Schmidt, K. (1998). Japanese TV ads: A video resource for the English discussion class. *The Language Teacher, 22*(8), 39. Retrieved from http://jalt-publications.org/tlt

Scifo, B. (2009). The sociocultural forms of mobile personal photographs in a cross-media ecology: Reflections starting from the young Italian experience. *Knowledge, Technology, and Politics, 22,* 185–194. doi:10.1007/s12130-009-9080-1

Shah, N. (2011). *Global camera phone sales to reach 1 billion in 2011.* Available from http://www.strategyanalytics.com/default.aspx?mod=reportabstractviewer&a0=6216

Sherman, J. (2003). *Using authentic video in the language classroom.* Cambridge, England: Cambridge University Press.

Skourtou, E., Kourtis-Kazoullis, V., & Cummins, J. (2006). Designing virtual learning environments for academic language development. In J. Weiss, J. Nolan, J. Hunsinger,. & P. Trifonas (Eds.), *The international handbook of virtual learning environments* (pp. 441–467). New York, NY: Springer.

Smidt, E., & Hegelheimer, V. (2004). Effects of online academic lectures on ESL listening comprehension, incidental vocabulary acquisition, and strategy use. *Computer Assisted Language Learning, 17,* 517–556. doi:10.1080/0958822042000319692

Smythe, S., & Toohey, K. (2009a). Bringing home and community to school: Institutional constraints and pedagogic possibilities. In J. Miller, A. Kostogriz, & M. Gearon (Eds.), *Culturally and linguistically diverse classrooms: New dilemmas for teachers* (pp. 271–290). Bristol, England: Multilingual Matters.

Smythe, S., & Toohey, K. (2009b). Investigating sociohistorical contexts and practices through a community scan: A Canadian Punjabi-Sikh example. *Language and Education, 21*(1), 37–57. doi:10.1080/09500780802152887

South, J. B., Gabbitas, B., & Merrill, P. F. (2008). Designing video narratives to contextualize content for ESL learners: A design process case study. *Interactive Learning Environments, 16*, 231–243. doi:10.1080/10494820802114044

Stahl, S. A., & Nagy, W. E. (2006). *Teaching word meanings*. Mahwah, NJ: Lawrence Erlbaum.

Stake, R. (2000). Case studies. In N. Denzin & Y. Lincoln (Eds.), *Handbook of qualitative research* (2nd ed., pp. 435–454). Thousand Oaks, CA: Sage.

Stanovich, K. E. (1986). Matthew effects in reading: Some consequences of individual differences in the acquisition of literacy. *Reading Research Quarterly, 21*, 360–407. doi:10.1598/RRQ.21.4.1

Statistics Canada. (2005, March 22). Study: Canada's visible minority population in 2017. *The Daily*. Retrieved from http://www.statcan.gc.ca/daily-quotidien/050322/dq050322b-eng.htm

Statistics Canada. (2010). *University enrolments by program level and instructional program*. Retrieved from http://www.statcan.gc.ca/tables-tableaux/sum-som/l01/cst01/educ54a-eng.htm

Statistics Canada. (2011). *College enrolment*. Retrieved from http://www.statcan.gc.ca/daily-quotidien/090505/dq090505c-eng.htm

Statistics. (n.d.). Retrieved from http://www.youtube.com/t/press_statistics

Stein, P. (2004). Representation, rights, and resources: Multimodal pedagogies in the language and literacy classroom. In B. Norton & K. Toohey (Eds.), *Critical pedagogies and language learning* (pp. 95–115). Cambridge, England: Cambridge University Press.

Steinberg, B., & Kelly, T. (1986). *True colors*. Retrieved from http://www.risa.co.uk/sla/song.php?songid=16568

Stempleski, S. (1992). Teaching communication skills with authentic video. In S. Stempleski & P. Arcario (Eds.), *Video in second language teaching: Using, selecting, and producing video for the classroom* (pp. 7–24). Alexandria, VA: TESOL.

Stempleski, S., & Arcario, P. (1992). *Video in second language teaching: Using, selecting, and producing video for the classroom*. Alexandria, VA: TESOL.

Stockwell, G. (2010). Using mobile phones for vocabulary activities: Examining the effect of the platform. *Language learning & technology, 14*(2), 95–110. Retrieved from http://llt.msu.edu/vol14num2/stockwell.pdf

Street, B. (1984). *Literacy in theory and practice*. Cambridge, England: Cambridge University Press.

Street, B. (1995). *Social literacies: Critical approaches to literacy, development, ethnography and education*. Boston, MA: Addison-Wesley.

Street, B. (1998). New literacies in theory and practice: What are the implications for language in education? *Linguistics and Education, 10*(1), 1–24.

Swaffer, J., & Vlatten, A. (1997). A sequential model for video viewing in the foreign language curriculum. *Modern Language Journal, 81,* 175–188. doi:10.1111/j.1540-4781.1997.tb01173.x

Swain, M. (1985). Communicative competence: Some roles of comprehensible input and comprehensible output in its development. In S. Gass & C. Madden (Eds.), *Input in second language acquisition* (pp. 235–256). New York, NY: Newberry House.

Swain, M. (2005). The output hypothesis: Theory and research. In E. Hinkel (Ed.), *Handbook of second language teaching and learning* (pp. 471–484). New York, NY: Routledge.

Template Ready. (n.d.). *PowerPoint tutorial.* Retrieved from http://windows .microsoft.com/en-US/windows-live/movie-maker-get-started

Toffler, A. (1980). *The third wave.* New York, NY: William Morrow.

Toohey, K. (2000). *Learning English at school: Identity, social relations and classroom practice.* Bristol, England: Multilingual Matters.

Triggs, P., & John, P. (2004). From transaction to transformation: Information and communication technology, professional development and the formation of communities of practice. *Journal of Computer Assisted Learning, 20,* 426–439. doi:10.1111/j.1365-2729.2004.00101.x

Uzunboylu, H., Cavus, N., & Ercag, E. (2009). Using mobile learning to increase environmental awareness. *Computers & Education, 52,* 381–389. doi:10.1016/ j.compedu.2008.09.008

Vanderplank, R. (1993). A very verbal medium: Language learning through closed captions. *TESOL Journal, 3*(1), 10–14.

Vanderplank, R. (2010). Déjà vu? A decade of research on language laboratories, television and video in language learning. *Language Teaching, 43,* 1–37. doi:10.1017/ S0261444809990267

Vygotsky, L. S. (1978). *Mind in society: The development of higher psychology process.* Cambridge, MA: Harvard University Press.

Wagner, E. (2007). Are they watching? Test-taker viewing behavior during an L2 video listening test. *Language Learning & Technology, 11*(1), 67–86. Retrieved from http://llt.msu.edu/

Wagner, E. (2008). Video listening tests: What are they measuring? *Language Assessment Quarterly, 5,* 218–243. doi:10.1080/15434300802213015

Wagner, E. (2010). The effect of the use of video texts on ESL listening test-taker performance. *Language Testing, 27,* 493–513. doi:10.1177/0265532209355668

Walks, R., & Bourne, L. (2006). Ghettos in Canada's cities? Racial segregation, ethnic enclaves and poverty concentration in Canadian urban areas. *Canadian Geographer, 50*, 273–297. doi:10.1111/j.1541-0064.2006.00142.x

Warschauer, M. (2011). *Learning in the cloud: How (and why) to transform schools with digital media.* New York, NY: Teachers College Press.

Wertsch, J. (1998). *Mind as action.* New York, NY: Oxford University Press.

West, M. (1953). *A general service list of English words.* London, England: Longman, Green.

Whiting, J., & Granoff, S. (2010). The effects of multimedia input on comprehension of a short story. *TESL-EJ, 14*(2), 1–10. Retrieved from http://www .tesl-ej.org/wordpress/

Wilcox, B. L., Kunkel, D., Cantor, J., Dowrick, P., Linn, S., & Palmer, E. (2004). *Report of the APA Task Force on Advertising and Children.* Washington, DC: American Psychological Association. Retrieved from http://www.apa.org/pi/families /resources/advertising-children.pdf

Yildiz, M. (2008). *Teachers discovering media education: Integrating videos into social studies curriculum.* Retrieved from http://citation.allacademic.com/meta/p_mla _apa_research_citation/0/3/6/3/6/pages36365/p36365-1.php

About the Editors and Contributors

EDITORS

Jia Li is an assistant professor in the Faculty of Education at the University of Ontario Institute of Technology and a Canada-U.S. Fulbright Scholar at the Harvard Graduate School of Education. Upon receiving her PhD in second language education from Ontario Institute for Studies in Education at the University of Toronto, she conducted her postdoctoral research at the Faculty of Education of Queen's University and taught at York University as an adjunct professor. Her research interests include emerging technologies for language and literacy development and innovative instructional design for linguistically diverse students.

Nicolas Gromik teaches at the National University of Singapore. He has also taught English at Tohoku University in Japan and Qatar University. His research interests are centered on the application of multimedia and mobile technology in the ESOL classroom, including the use of video production to enhance listening comprehension and speaking skills for ESL and EFL students. He is currently completing his PhD studies in education and technology at James Cook University, in Australia. His thesis research focuses on mobile-assisted language learning.

Nicholas Edwards works at iDiscoveri Education, in Gurgaon, India, where he leads the design of technology-integrated educational programs for nonnative English learning among K–8 students in India. He received his EdM in language and literacy from the Harvard Graduate School of Education. His research interests include constructivist pedagogy, experiential learning, ESL/EFL, and the use of technology for ESL/EFL learning. He taught English as a nonnative language in South Korea and the United States.

CONTRIBUTORS

James Cummins (Preface) is a professor in the Department of Curriculum, Teaching, and Learning at Ontario Institute for Studies in Education (OISE), University of Toronto, and a Canada Research Chair (Tier I) in Language Learning and Literacy Development in Multilingual Contexts. A recipient of the International Reading Association's Albert J. Harris award and an honorary doctorate in Humane Letters from the Bank Street College of Education in New York City, in recent years, Dr. Cummins has been involved in projects on multiliteracies, assessment, and the academic trajectory of ELLs.

Joyce Cunningham teaches at Ibaraki University in Japan. She was a column coeditor for *The Language Teacher*, published by the Japan Association for Language Teaching.

Diane Dagenais is a professor in the Faculty of Education of Simon Fraser University, in Burnaby, Canada.

Allyson Eamer is an assistant professor in the Faculty of Education at the University of Ontario Institute of Technology, in Oshawa, Canada.

Janette Hughes is an associate professor in the Faculty of Education at the University of Ontario Institute of Technology, in Oshawa, Canada.

Jingjing Jiang is a program coordinator at Primary Source, a nonprofit professional development organization that promotes global education, in Boston, Massachusetts. She received her EdM in language and literacy from the Harvard Graduate School of Education.

Peizhao Li is a college preparation consultant and the assistant director of C2 Education, in New York City. She received her EdM in language and literacy from the Harvard Graduate School of Education.

Heather Lotherington is a professor in the Faculty of Education of York University, in Toronto, Canada.

Brenda McComb is an assistant professor in the Department of Languages, Literatures, and Linguistics at York University, in Toronto, Canada.

Natalia Sinitskaya Ronda holds a research position at the Council of Ministers of Education, in Toronto, Canada. She received her PhD from the Faculty of Education of York University, in Toronto, Canada.

Kelleen Toohey is a professor and associate dean in the Faculty of Education of Simon Fraser University, in Burnaby, Canada.

Aiden Yeh is an assistant professor at Wenzao Ursuline College of Languages, in Kaohsiung, Taiwan. She received her PhD in applied linguistics from Birmingham University, in England.

Index

Page numbers followed by an *f* or *t* indicate figures or tables.

A

Academic language, 119, 121, 125, 132
Acculturation, 87
Accuracy in language production, 139–140
Active practice, 106–108
Adjectives, 59
Adverbs, 59
Advertisement projects. *See also* Multimedia
  projects regarding advertisements
  case studies illustrating, 104–113
  literature review, 102–104
  overview, 5–6, 101–102, 113–115
Agency, 49–50
Analysis, 59
Applications of digital media, 2–3
Apps, 11
Assessment
  advertisement projects and, 109–110
  photostory projects and, 70–71, 71*f*
Authentic materials, 140–141
Awareness, 86

B

Basic interpersonal communication skills
  (BICS), 119, 121, 132
Blended learning environment
  cell phone video project and, 118
  photostory projects and, 64–65
Blogging, 65

C

Camera phones, 1–2. *See also* Cell phones
Captions, 141–144
Case studies
  advertisement projects and, 104–113
  cell phone video project and, 120–132,
    122*t*, 127*f*
  communicative competence and, 19–29,
    24*f*, 26*f*, 27*f*, 28*f*
  digital storytelling and identity
    construction, 51–60, 56*f*, 57*f*, 58*f*, 60*f*,
    61*f*
  filmmaking project and, 92–97, 95*t*, 97*t*
  overview, 4–5
  photostory projects, 73–76, 73*t*
  videomaking project, 36–45, 40*f*, 41*f*, 43*f*
Cell phone video project. *See also* Cell phones;
  Filmmaking projects
  case studies illustrating, 120–132, 122*t*, 127*f*
  limitations, 130–131
  literature review, 117–119
  overview, 117, 120–121, 132–133
  theoretical framework, 119–120, 119*t*
Cell phones, 1–2, 117–118. *See also* Camera
  phones; Cell phone video project; Text
  messaging
Citizenship, 87
Classroom environment, 64–65, 118
Cognitive academic language proficiency
  (CALP), 119, 121, 125, 132
Collaboration
  advertisement projects and, 103
  collaborative authorship, 11, 16
  digital storytelling and identity
    construction and, 59
  filmmaking project and, 92–94
  overview, 30–31

Also Available From TESOL

More Than a Native Speaker

and

From Language Learner to Language Teacher
Don Snow

❋ ❋ ❋ ❋ ❋

TESOL Classroom Practice Series
Maria Dantas-Whitney, Sarah Rilling, and Lilia Savova, Series Editors

❋ ❋ ❋ ❋ ❋

Language Teacher Development Series
Thomas S. C. Farrell, Series Editor

❋ ❋ ❋ ❋ ❋

New Ways in TESOL Series
Jack C. Richards, Series Editor

❋ ❋ ❋ ❋ ❋

TESOL Language Curriculum Development Series
Kathleen Graves, Series Editor

❋ ❋ ❋ ❋ ❋

TESOL Standards

- *Preparing Effective Teachers of English Language Learners: Practical Applications for the TESOL P–12 Professional Teaching Standards*

- *Standards for Adult Education ESL Programs*

- *Standards for ESL/EFL Teachers of Adults*

- *TESOL Technology Standards: Description, Implementation, Integration*

- *PreK–12 English Language Proficiency Standards*
  Augmentation of the World-Class Instructional Design and Assessment (WIDA) Consortium English Language Proficiency Standards

To Order or Request a Review Copy

Online: www.tesol.org "Read and Publish"
Email: tesolpubs@brightkey.net
Toll Free Phone: +1 888-891-0041 (United States)
Mail: TESOL Publications, 9050 Junction Drive
Annapolis Junction, MD 20701 USA